Mountain and Moorland Ponies

of the British Isles

Peggy Grayson

Mrs Newbold Young with the Dartmoor stallion Bransby Cyclone in driving dressage.

Acknowledgements 4

Introduction 5

1 The Origins of the Native Ponies 6

2 Characteristics of the Native Ponies 10

3 The Romantic and Useful Exmoor 16

4 The Graceful and Dependable Dartmoor 26

5 The Hardy and Adaptable Highland 32

6 The Handy and Serviceable Shetland 38

7 The Efficient and Stylish Connemara 44

8 The Versatile and Useful New Forest 50

9 The Attractive and Adaptable Fell 58

10 The Durable and Steadfast Dales 64

11 Welsh Ponies and Cobs 70

12 Choosing the Right Breed 82

13 Cost of Pony and Maintenance 88

14 Basic Management 96

15 Shows and Showing 102

Useful Addresses 114

Suggested Reading 115

Glossary of Everyday Terms 116

Points of the Horse 128

Acknowledgements

Mrs Ash
Rachel Bell
Amanda Brown
Dr Wynne Davies
Mr Dougal Dick
Kath Girdler
Mrs A Halfpenny
Mrs E A Haycock
Mrs E House
Nicki Howard
Mr Lionel Hamilton Renwick
Mrs P Harvey Richards
Mr and Mrs R James
Mrs Kofteros

Miss Mary Longsdon
Mrs G Lowth
Miss Pat Lyne
Mr D Mansell
Mrs Newbolt Young
Nicholas Palmer
Mrs T Elliot Reep
Anthony Reynolds
Clive Richardson
Lady Luki Scott
Mr and Mrs Bernard Tidmarsh
Mrs Anne Vestey
Mrs J Webb
Misses Williams and Nash

The author and publishers would like to thank all the above for their help and kindness in supplying photographs.

The author and publishers would also like to thank Mrs Fitzgerald (Dales Pony Society), Mrs Penny Smith (Highlands) and Miss D Macnair (New Forest) who so kindly gave information as well as photographs.

Welsh Cob Kentchurch Chaos.

Introduction

In 1949, I met Mrs Glenda Spooner who first kindled my interest in the native pony. Her love for, and interest in, the mountain and moorland breeds unique to these islands led to the formation of Ponies of Britain. This group organised shows at which the native breeds, some in sad decline, could be seen and appreciated, and also gave rise to an urgently-needed welfare section for ponies of all kinds.

Many regard Mrs Spooner as the saviour of our wonderful native pony heritage for it was her drive and insight, coupled with her journalistic experience and flair for publicity, that inspired countless pony people to take up the cause of the mountain and moorland breeds, thereby ensuring their survival. This wider interest in all the native breeds led ultimately to the tremendous popularity they now enjoy.

With more leisure time available today, many people from non-horsey backgrounds take up riding as a hobby and then become determined to purchase their own mount. This book is for all those who want to learn more about our native breeds.

Chapter 1

The Origins of the Native Pony

The British native breeds of pony have all descended from the original animals that arrived in these islands thousands of years ago. There is a theory, quite well supported by scientific research, that during the Ice Age an enclave formed in Northern Europe in which various mammals, including small ponies, managed to survive until the Great Thaw. Then a trek westwards began which lasted several centuries, until ponies crossed the land bridge that then existed between the Continent and this island. Fossilised bones and teeth dug up in the area where the enclave is said to have existed and others found on Exmoor seem to confirm this theory, which is accepted by many experts.

In several ways, the Exmoor pony bears a resemblance to Przewalskii's horse, which is believed to be related to the original wild horse of the Mongolian plains. Its descendants live there today where they are known as Takis. These similarities also give credence to the enclave theory.

Over the years groups of ponies (then termed 'small horses') settled in various

Fell ponies Bewcastle Beacon, Bewcastle Bouquet and Bewcastle Bonny owned by Miss Longsdon and Mr Goddard.

areas of these islands. Gradually people tamed them and bred them to be of use for the various domestic tasks they were to perform. Their size and structure were governed by the climate and herbage available in their districts.

Various horses arrived from other countries, with merchants and travellers, as mounts for invading armies or as gifts for royalty and the ruling classes. Many of these breeds were crossed with the indigenous stock which, over the decades, broke down the various characteristics of the invaders and assimilated them to its own advantage, never losing its own strength, hardiness and character. (Alien blood was not only used in the distant past. In recent years, several of our native breeds have had to be crossed with stock of other breeds to ensure their survival when base stock ran low, mainly owing to the exigencies of war. Most crosses made in this century are recorded in the stud books of the various breeds.)

As time progressed and horses and ponies were bred to specific types desired for war, transport or sport, the breeds became more defined. It was the owners' careful selection of breeding stock that ensured our wonderful heritage of equines today.

In the distant past, Britain was largely forested but with tracts of moorland and mountain – wild, rugged, forbidding and roadless. The ponies of those times were used as pack animals, carrying food, firing, clothing and other essentials to those living in town and country alike.

Horses and ponies in the Middle Ages were unlikely to have been used on the primitive farms of the day as they were much too valuable, so the arable land was cultivated either by hand or by oxen. When ploughs and harrows became more sophisticated, horses and ponies were

taken for farm work and the slow oxen phased out. As tracks through the forests and over the moors widened and became roads, wheeled transport slowly began to take the place of the pack horses and

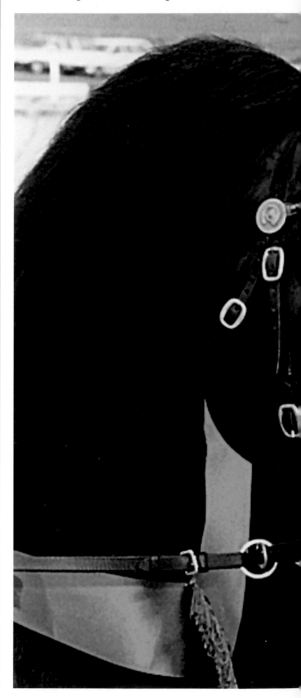

ponies which were then put in the shafts. Until well into the 20th century, much of the commerce of this country was carried by horse-drawn vehicles.

Woven like a tapestry into the history of these islands is the history of the mountain and moorland ponies.

Welsh Section B stallions Mark Oak Atlantis (left) and Mark Oak Adante (right). Photograph by Anthony Reynolds.

Chapter 2

Characteristics of the Native Pony

The definition of a mountain and moorland pony is: 'One whose ancestors have lived on mountain, moor or common for the last three generations in semi-feral conditions.'

It is this definition that requires private breeders to go back every so often to source, either for females to bring into their lines or for young mountain- or moor-bred colts who can come on for use as stallions. Failure to do this could result in breeds losing their mountain and moorland status, and also mean that many breed characteristics could be lost, especially the ability to survive in poor conditions and severe weather.

The native breeds have many things in common. They are shorter on the leg and longer in the body than the thoroughbred pony, whose ratio of height to length is the reverse of the native. They are all well-boned and of sturdy constitution, their intellect is keen, they abound in concentrated vitality. Durability is their middle name. They have large eyes and small ears. Their feet are good-sized and well-shaped with hard horn. They have well-muscled forearms, short cannons,

Siskin, a champion Exmoor, owned by Mrs J Webb. Photograph by Sally Ann Thomson

Trowan Bonny Lassie, a Highland pony owned by Mrs Sandoe and Mrs Lowners.
Photograph by Anthony Reynolds.

In each breed heads are every bit as distinctive as the movement and size that were determined long ago by the terrain on which the pony lived, the climate, and the herbage available for survival and the work it was expected to perform.

That some breeds have had their heights altered in comparatively recent times is just another step in the history of the natives. Nothing stands still and, as the need for the pony solely as a workhorse or a means of transport is lost, its place in modern Britain is as a vehicle for the pursuit of leisure and pleasure. Therefore it is altering slowly but surely every year as the tasks it is expected to perform change and increase.

The reduction in the amount of natural hacking country and the danger on the roads force much horse work to be taken in small fields and covered schools. This has led to more and more owners of native ponies competing in some form of equestrian sport, if only to get away from the monotony of endless circles.

Native ponies are, by their very nature, free spirits. They need the stimulus of work and excitement and quickly get bored and sluggish if not fully extended. It is as well to bear all this in mind when deciding to buy a specimen of one of the native breeds.

Why buy a native pony? Well, the advantages are many. It has a more robust constitution than the thoroughbred pony,

good knees, well-rounded quarters and strong hocks. Their thick, sweeping manes and tails and heavy winter coats insulate them against the worst of the weather. The standard of points for each breed encompasses these general attributes and also gives details of the required size, head shape and mode of locomotion. These last three separate one breed from another. A Highland pony moving like a Welsh cob is not acceptable, any more than is a Dartmoor with an Exmoor's distinct head, or a Shetland the size of a Welsh Mountain pony.

Mrs V James' Dales pony, Abdylane Susie.

and does not need the same quality or amount of grazing or the same amount of short feed and hay as a horse. It can stay out longer in bad weather conditions, does not need so many expensive visits from the vet, is (in the main) easier to break and handle, and the majority are useful for all members of the family. Apart from all that, there is the interest of owning a breed with a fascinating history.

Native ponies can do all the work that any other pony can do, and possibly do it better. They can take their place alongside horses when it comes to hunting, driving and hacking. Nowadays, the native breeds take part in every equine discipline and perform with ease in the highly-competitive modern Pony Club.

The Committees of agricultural, horse and pony shows and the pony societies

Dartmoor Hisley Pedlar, photographed by Carol Gilson.

Section A Welsh Mountain pony, Bengad Wild Indigo, photographed by Eberhard Holin.

mad children, do think carefully before buying that longed-for pony. Children have to go to school and therefore parents end up as the stable hands. If you have no knowledge, you cannot do the job properly and it has to be done come rain or shine if the animal is not to suffer.

Let the children go to a good riding school where they can be taught not only riding but some stable management, and member-ship of the Pony Club will help enormously. There are often gatherings which parents can attend and, by mixing with more experi-enced people, you can educate yourself in the proper care of ponies. You will be ready to succumb to the pleas of, "Can I have a pony of my own, please?" confident that you have the knowledge to support the young rider.

quickly recognised that owners of mountain and moorland ponies wanted the same level of competition as that available to the owners of thoroughbreds, and speedily devised sections in all disciplines with exciting championships. These classes are now among the best supported at shows up and down the country.

People with limited means and accommodation will find the native pony ideal for hacking and possibly hunting, as a pony for the children, as a family mount and/or as a driving pony.

Although I have stressed that a native breed is hardy and strong, it does need the correct care and maintenance, and cannot be turned out and forgotten until someone decides he or she wants to ride it.

To parents, especially those with no experience of horses but who have pony-

Ynsfaen Lady Barnaby, Welsh Section D. Photograph by Anthony Reynolds.

Chapter 3

The Romantic and Useful Exmoor

History of the breed

Take a good look at the Exmoor for surely it has a romantic past. It may even be a descendant of the first ponies to settle in these islands for, having been threatened with extinction several times over the years, it has proved one of the hardiest of survivors.

Exmoor is a wild and rugged place even in this sophisticated day and age. Think how it must have looked two or more centuries ago, with its few lonely cottages and wayside inns, and its rocky, forbidding coastline pierced by little inlets where small craft could land illicit cargoes on dark nights. Smuggling along the coast was a way of life for many villagers, and be sure that Rudyard Kipling's 'four and twenty ponies trotting through the dark', and many more besides, came off the Moor to be used in the transport of contraband. Look at the broad back, big shoulders, long, silent walk and effortless trot of the modern Exmoor and it is not hard to imagine it as an ideal pony for the smuggler.

Anchor herd of Exmoor mares and foals on Winsford Hill. Photograph by Dr Sue Baker.

The Exmoor has always been renowned for its strength in ratio to its size. William Youatt in *The Horse*, published in 1859, has this to say:

The Exmoor ponies, although ugly enough, are hardy and useful. A well-known sportsman says he rode one of them half a dozen miles, and never felt such power and action in so small a compass before. To show his accomplishments he was turned (jumped) over a gate at least eight inches higher than his back, and his owner, who rides fourteen stone, travelled on his from Bristol to South Molton, sixty-eight miles, beating the coach which runs the same road.

wheeled cart or possibly a sledge, that is, several boughs tied together in a large V, on which hay, corn and dung could be transported over the stony tracks. The farmer would have found the Exmoor pony useful for shepherding and both he and his wife would have ridden and later driven their ponies to and from market. At one time there was a breed called the Devon Pack Horse, which was a cross of the Exmoor with larger animals. The breed died out some time ago but for many years was used in the West Country for transport.

Exmoor was a Royal Forest with the

Knightcombe Burnished Brass to a four-wheeled competition phaeton driven by Mrs Melanie Wright.

Of course the Exmoor had many uses other than as a riding animal for the better-off moorland folk. On the small farms it would have pulled a rough, two-

customary grazing rights, but in 1818 it was deforested and partially enclosed. The Warden of the Forest, Sir James Acland, was granted 3000 acres for the

Everyone can enjoy the Midsummer ride.

loss of his post as Warden. He drove about 400 of his ponies onto his estate and this, together with the activity of the moorland farmers who bought stock at the dispersal sale, saved this historic breed for future generations. Sir Richard's 'Anchor' brand is still in use today by his descendants.

Two World Wars decimated the ponies on Exmoor. Many went for slaughter and, when the military was stationed there during the last war, the ponies were used as moving targets by practising marksmen.

In the 1950s the breed featured on the endangered species list and its cause was espoused by the Rare Breeds Survival Trust. Happily the Exmoor pony's unique history, appearance and great usefulness were recognised and many new owners joined with those people who had fought for its survival. Today the spread of the breed across the country is quite remarkable.

Characteristics of the Exmoor

The Exmoor pony is very distinctive and not liable to be confused with any other breed. The mares do not exceed 12.2 hh although the stallions and geldings may go up to 12.3 hh. They are always bay or brown, or what is known as an 'Exmoor dun' which is a little lighter than bay.

Pair jumping with Exmoor ponies.

Exmoor ponies and their riders enjoying the Easter Egg Challenge race, photographed by Mrs P Webb.

Their legs, mane and tail are black. They are distinguished by mealy-coloured markings on the muzzle, round the eyes, inside the flanks and under the belly. All registered Exmoors are branded with a star on the nearside shoulder and a number under this indicates the herd to which they belong. On the quarter on the same side is another number which is the distinguishing number for the pony within the herd. A pony with these brands can be said to 'bear its breeding on its back', as all foals are examined by breed experts and have to be correct in all breed details before they are accepted for branding. Ponies described as Exmoor but without this branding may be pure-bred but have some fault which renders them unsuitable for registration, or they might be cross-bred. Any white markings on an Exmoor is a fault, except for the freeze-branding numbers that show up as white, usually in the saddle region. This mark is put on to help identify ponies should they be lost or stolen.

The head of the Exmoor is distinctive, being wide between the eyes and short in the muzzle with large, open nostrils and deep jaws. One of the breed characteristics is the 'toad eye': a bony ridge or brow which protects the large, well-shaped eyes from damage from the icy rain and snow. The ears are short, thick, pointed and well furred inside, again as protection against the weather.

Exmoors are sturdily boned with well-formed joints, short, strong cannons and hard, well-shaped feet. They are stronger and a little thicker in the neck than other natives of comparable size, and the neck runs down to join a wide, well-shaped chest. There is great depth through the girth allowing for plenty of heart and lung room, a strong back and loin, and large, well-rounded quarters. The tail is furnished with an abundance of hair and set at a point where the buttocks meet, and in bad weather is pressed tight between the buttocks. At the root of the tail the hair should fan out over the buttocks

Exmoors look well ridden side saddle.
Photograph courtesy of Helen Knowles.

producing what is known as the 'snow shute' which enables the accumulated snow and water to slide off. The mane is thick and long and there is a heavy forelock, again as a protection against bad weather.

The winter coat of the Exmoor consists of a close undercoat and long, greasy top coat which is quite weatherproof. Together with whorls on the quarters, these features enable rain and snow to slide off, leaving the pony's body warm and dry. In spring, the ponies moult their winter jackets and display a fine, sleek summer coat that with good grooming shines a rich colour. They require little preparation for a show as neither mane nor tail should be trimmed or plaited, but brushed out well and tidied.

The Exmoor is a self-sufficient pony; its history is that of a born survivor and it thinks it knows what is best for it! You need patience and perseverance to encourage an Exmoor to enjoy the schooling necessary to make it an obedient and enjoyable ride. It can be stubborn and needs to be coaxed – do not try to pit your will against this pony as it will win every time! Show it how much better it is to do things your way and you will have little trouble; once the pony starts to enjoy the work you will find it most willing.

Although small and quite heavily built, the Exmoor has a fair turn of speed and many have been successfully ridden to hounds on their native heath.

For a family that wants a pony strong enough to carry the adults as well as the children, Exmoors are ideal. They also break well to harness and so have potential as ride and drive ponies. However, it must be remembered that the Exmoor is a small pony and, although strong enough for adults, only shorter people look really right on top. If the adult is over 1.6m (5ft 5in), one of the larger native breeds may be more suitable.

As an all-round pony, the Exmoor is hard to beat. As a rule, it is very good on modern roads and is intelligent enough to keep out of danger. It seems to have a particular empathy with the disadvantaged; many Exmoors have been used to teach the disabled to ride and drive and they look after their charges with extreme care and kindness.

Care must be taken with the feeding. Too much green grass or short feed not only makes the Exmoor put on weight which is very difficult to get off, but can lead to laminitis or 'fever in the feet', as some call this very painful, and sometimes fatal, disease. All native ponies are prone to laminitis if they are kept on too good a diet and it is essential to have controlled grazing and a well-thought-out short feed and hay programme for an Exmoor that is in constant work.

Exmoor ponies are a fairly trouble-free breed if kept well, and will give their owners many years of work and devotion. Those who buy a filly or mare may, in time, decide to breed a foal rather than part with her. Consult someone who knows the bloodlines and can advise on a suitable stallion. Exmoor mares put to a (small) Hunter Improvement stallion have bred excellent cross-country animals and hunters up to about 15.2 hh.

schooled to jump very well, but you should not expect a show jumper. Natural fences are more in their line and they perform with distinction across country, being very bold and sure-footed. They are safe and reliable as hacks or for hunting.

The affairs of the breed are managed by the Exmoor Pony Society which was founded in 1921 (see Useful Addresses). The annual breed show is at Exford in August.

At shows there are classes solely for the breed, and they can also go in the small section of the mixed mountain and moorland in hand and ridden classes and Working Hunter Pony. The latter provides an exciting change for both rider and mount. Many Exmoors have been

Nutcracker and Catriona on a long-distance ride. Photograph courtesy of D. Mansell.

Pages 22–23: champion Exmoor mare Redsyke and her foal. Photograph by Sally Ann Thomson.

Chapter 4

The Graceful and Dependable Dartmoor

History of the breed

Dartmoor is still a wild and beautiful place and it has been recorded that ponies have grazed there for over 900 years. The first mention of them appears in the reign of Bishop Aelfwold in 1012. Two centuries later there is another reference to the ponies as costing 2d (about 1p) a head to pasture on the moor.

Little more known history is recorded until the coming of tin mining and the ponies played a big part in this industry. When the mines were worked out, the ponies were turned back to the moor.

In 1859 Youatt wrote: *There is on Dartmoor a race of ponies much in request in that vicinity, being sure footed and hardy, and admirably calculated to scramble over the rough roads and dreary wilds of that mountainous district. The Dartmoor pony is larger than the Exmoor, and if possible, uglier. He exists there almost in a state of nature.*

The Dartmoor breed has come a long way since Youatt wrote this rather unflattering description!

Langfield Miz Sophie and Kellie Heppenstall show ease and style over a Working Hunter pony jump.

No doubt the Dartmoor, like the Exmoor, played its part in smuggling contraband and it was surely used as a pack pony by the 'wreckers', those people who waded out to ships smashed on the rocks of the formidable coastline to salvage what they could find of the cargo.

Farmers on the moor have used the Dartmoor pony both for tillage and transport over the years, and at one time

Dartmoor has to compete for its livelihood with the demands of tourism and increased road widening and building. Each year, for one reason or another, more ground is lost. Apart from that, not all ponies on the moor are pure Dartmoor. A number of small bands of alien animals are turned out in various areas which increases the demand for natural herbage.

Over the decades, many who live on

Shilstone Rocks Mercury and his mares grazing on Dartmoor. Photograph by Tracey Elliot-Reep.

warders from the prison rode these ponies when they accompanied groups of prisoners to work in the local quarries.

After the First World War, the numbers and quality of the ponies fell considerably, and other blood had to be imported in order to preserve the breed. Nearly all the present-day ponies descend from a stallion called 'The Leat', who was a son of the desert-bred Arab, 'Dwarka'.

Like all semi-feral grazers, the

the moor have kept and nurtured the breed, but the grace and symmetry of line of the Dartmoor pony, its biddable nature and hardiness have endeared it to pony owners and breeders world-wide. There are famous and successful studs of Dartmoor ponies not only in its native county, but all over the United Kingdom and overseas. The well-known established studs in Devon have ponies both running the moor and in home paddocks.

Characteristics of the Dartmoor

At one time the height of this pony was 14 hh for stallions and 13.2 hh for mares. Few measured that height, with most being around 13.1 hh. Today the maximum height allowed is 12.2 hh.

The Dartmoor pony has been likened to a hunter in miniature and, indeed, it does resemble its larger cousin with its small, blood-like head, open nostrils and large, bright eyes. It must, however, have small, pony ears neatly set and alert. It is clean throated, with a strong yet elegant neck that fits into well-laid 'riding' shoulders. The body is of medium length, well ribbed with a good depth of girth. Loin and quarters are strong and well muscled and the tail well set up. The Dartmoor stands on strong, flat boned legs, its knees are well developed and flat, its pasterns sloping. It has the round, well-shaped tough feet of its ancestors. It moves with a free-flowing action but with no exaggeration. Mane, forelock and tail are abundant and with quality hair. The Dartmoor may be brown, black, grey, chestnut or roan. Piebald and skewbald are not allowed, and excessive white markings are discouraged.

The general appearance is of a typical native pony of quality. Like all native ponies, the Dartmoor puts on excess weight if the grazing is too abundant or it is overfed in any way. With its kind nature and good build the Dartmoor is an ideal children's pony but, as it is strongly built and has good bone and limbs, it is up to a bit of weight and often is ridden in the

Dartmoor ponies are suitable for all ages of rider. Langfield Dragon's Rock and his young rider in a 1st Novice Ridden competition.

show ring by small adults. As a family pony it can be exercised when the young riders are at school.

Dartmoors make good Pony Club mounts as they are sensible, able and willing, free natural jumpers and do not get over-excited. They are excellent for Nursery and Cradle Stakes, Working Hunter Pony and Hunter Trials. They are well classified at shows and can be in the mixed mountain and moorland leading rein and first ridden classes as well as the open classes for this category, and are most successful in native ridden classes. Being kind and biddable they are good schoolmasters for youngsters learning to ride. Surefooted over country, they make good hunting ponies, and are pleasant hacks and companions for the non-competitive child or lightweight adult, and are very careful with the more nervous. Dartmoors break well to harness and make very smart driving ponies.

Once the Dartmoor mare has been outgrown by her young rider, she makes a good brood mare, and can be used to breed pure Dartmoors or, put to a thoroughbred or Arab, she will breed a good stamp of animal up to about 15.2 hh. Dartmoor mares put to a thoroughbred pony stallion have, over the years, bred some very successful children's riding ponies for the show ring. However, consult with someone knowledgeable who can advise on a suitable stallion.

Above: Sarah Goodman sets a fine but controlled pace with Huntspath Heath in a one-day event.
Photograph by Equestrian Services Thorney.

Left: Dartmoor foals have great charm. Ryland Castanet with her foal, Calina, and Langfield Chanel with Cashmere.
Photograph by Carol Gilson.

The breed's affairs are managed by the Dartmoor Pony Society, founded in 1925. It maintains the stud book, attends to registrations and keeps a sales list. The Society runs three annual shows and has an award scheme to promote the breeding and showing of Dartmoors.

Chapter 5

The Hardy and Adaptable Highland

History of the breed

The Highland pony owes some of its history to the Nordic breeds, and this shows in its wide range of attractive colours. The breed is mentioned in 13th century manuscripts, and at one time there were distinct varieties on the islands of Barra, Mull, Tiree, Erriskay, Rhum and Arran, where they worked on the crofts as well as being the sole means of transport for the islanders. These island breeds were smaller and lighter than their mainland brethren and have largely died out.

Youatt had this to say: *The Highland pony is far inferior to the Galloway. The head is large; he is low before and long in the back, short in the legs; upright in the pasterns and not a pleasant ride except at the canter. His habits make him hardy for he is seldom housed in the summer or winter.*

In *Travels in Scotland*, The Rev Mr Hall says, *when these animals come to any boggy piece of ground, they first put their nose to it, then pat it in a peculiar way with one of their forefeet; and from the sound and feel of the ground, they know whether it will bear them. They will do the same with ice, and determine in a minute whether they will proceed.*

Highlands make untiring driving ponies.

The Highland has been much favoured by great men. Robert the Bruce is said to have had one as his mount in the 14th century. When Dr Samuel Johnson made his famous progress on horseback with James Boswell round the mainland of Scotland much, if not all, was made on Highland ponies. It is recorded in *A Journey round Scotland* that some of these were loaned to the travellers by the Duke of Argyll. Robert Burns, the poet, refers to his 'Highland filly', but whether it had two or four legs is unclear!

Highlands have captured the imagination and affections of royalty. Queen Victoria kept some of this Highland breed at Balmoral where, no doubt, they were used not only to convey Her Majesty about the estate (for the Queen was a splendid horsewoman), but were probably in use as driving ponies

Nashend Sea Lavender on a sponsored ride.

when she was older. King George V had a favourite Highland pony he rode when he was at Balmoral for the shooting. Queen Elizabeth II still keeps a stud of Highlands at her Scottish home.

In Victorian times painters, notably Landseer, transferred many scenes of the Scottish landscape onto their canvases and a large number of these depicted Highland ponies at work or rest.

The Highland ponies were very popular with the sportsmen who went north for the shooting and deer stalking, for their comfortable, broad backs and sure-footedness provided transport for the less hardy. A number of ponies in each party would carry the saddle (or cradle) on which the slain stags would be strapped for conveyance down the mountain. Some ponies carried large wicker panniers, one on each side, to hold the sportsmen's food and equipment and were also used to carry the day's bag of birds during the grouse shooting season.

Highlands worked as pack animals, carrying goods about the rugged Scottish landscape before there was anything more than rough tracks over moor or mountain. They were reliable mounts for the shepherds. When roads were made they took to the shafts, and were also used on the crofts to pull ploughs and harrows and draw timber.

In this present day landowners have begun to realise the damage modern vehicles are inflicting on the terrain, so the ponies are once again out on the mountains and moors with the sportsmen during the season, carrying on the traditions of their ancestors. Although some Highland ponies do still work on crofts, their uses have gone far beyond the menial tasks of yesteryear.

In the last century, gentlemen of means, such as the Duke of Atholl, took

The Highland has no trouble navigating a Hunter Trial course. Photograph by Mike Freeman.

up the breed and selected animals to found formal studs. In the 1880s the Department of Agriculture established a stud of good type stallions at Inverness for the crofters to use on their mares.

Characteristics of the Highland

The Highland pony measures from 13 hh to 14.2 hh and comes in a variety of attractive colours inherited from its Nordic ancestors. Common are all shades of dun, yellow, gold, fox, mouse, cream and grey, with a dorsal stripe (called an eel stripe) down the spine, and zebra stripes on the legs. Brown, black and grey are allowed but not skewbald or piebald. Although they are animals of great substance, Highlands are ponies in all respects with the well-made pony head, rounded cheek bone, shortness from eye to nostrils which are large and open, broad forehead, and well set, large, kind eyes. The ears are small, well set and furred within.

The neck is powerful and of good length, nicely arched and well set into sloping shoulders. Powerful forearms are placed well under the body, the knees are broad, cannons well honed and short, and the feet large and particularly well shaped, with hard horn. There is a great depth of girth and good withers and a strong back with a natural curve, giving a 'good place for a saddle'. The quarters are large, powerful and well rounded, with well developed thighs and strong hocks. The mane and tail are long and flowing and of great beauty. Neither should be trimmed or pulled, but kept well brushed. The feather round the hoof is silky and ends in a prominent tuft on the fetlock.

Highland mares at Nashend Stud – a study in beauty and strength.

In winter the ponies grow a thick topcoat over a dense undercoat and seldom appear to feel the cold.

Because of its equable temperament, the Highland pony is usually easy to break and school on quietly. It is a wise and normally sedate individual, but willing to take part in any discipline put to it. Because of its kind nature and care of the humans in its company, the Highland has proved invaluable in the many trekking centres that have sprung up, and people who have never ridden before have been able to enjoy the beauties of Scotland and other districts from the safety of its comfortable back. It is in great demand for riding and driving for the disabled, being reliable in all situations.

The diversity in type and size makes the breed suitable for almost any kind of work. Many are fine jumpers across country, and some have distinguished themselves in the cross country driving events.

Although Highland ponies are given classes at shows all over the United Kingdom, to see the breed in any quantity it is still necessary to go to Scotland. At the Royal Highland Show over 100 Highlands are on view: a magnificent sight. Every second year the breed show is held at the Three Counties showground at Malvern in Worcestershire on the day following the two-day National Pony Show in the first week of August. Here the best of the breed can be seen in hand, ridden and driven.

The smaller ponies are ideal for active young people who want a pony for

Highland foals have plenty of charm and cheek!

harness that they can be driven just for pleasure or in any type of competition and make excellent ride and drive animals. In Scotland, shows classify classes for Highland ponies working on the large estates.

Highlands away from their native terrain do well on rough grazing and seem impervious to the weather, but do need shelter from extreme heat and flies. If good quality pasture is used, owners must take care not to let them get too fat. Treated well and regularly used, they have a long and healthy life.

Pedigree records have been kept since 1896. The Highland Pony Society was founded in 1923 and attends to the registrations and all the other affairs of the breed. It also publishes the annual Stud Book. The Highland Pony Enthusiasts' Club is based south of the border and has an active membership.

hunting, hacking and Pony Club work that is quiet and kind enough for them to look after without parental supervision.

All sizes, with their good build, strong flat bones and sound feet, are ideal mounts for adult riders, who can have much enjoyment hacking or hunting, long distance riding or riding club work. In the show sphere they compete in breed classes, family pony and Working Hunter pony. In the past, the farmer would have ridden to market with his wife sitting sideways on a pad behind him, and maybe this is why the Highland pony has taken so kindly to the side saddle. A number of riders have appeared with success in side saddle events, with both pony and rider looking exceedingly elegant and efficient.

Highlands do well in Hunter Trials and they take so readily to

Nashend Donald going freely over Working Hunter Pony jumps.

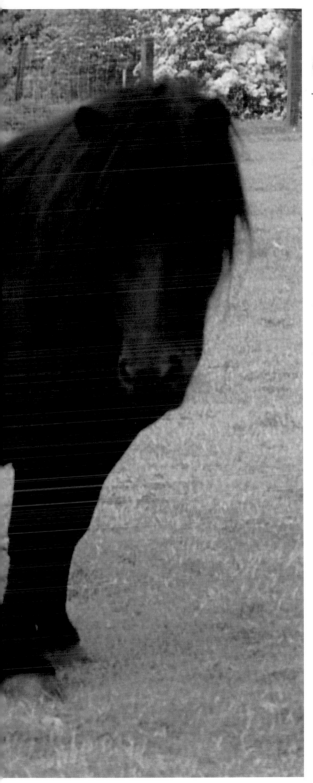

Chapter 6

The Hardy and Serviceable Shetland

History of the breed

Smallest of all the native breeds is the Shetland, whose roots go far back into the mists of time. The belief is that it lived and bred in the Scottish islands before the Norse invasion of the 8th and 9th centuries.

At one time it was thought that the Shetland was a small horse whose development had been stunted by lack of forage. On the island of Burra a stone was discovered and dated as being from the 9th century. This depicted a monk mounted on a small equine, and it was then concluded that the Shetland had always been this size and was a genuine native pony.

In 1859 Youatt wrote, *The Shetland pony, called in Scotland, the 'sheltie', an inhabitant of the extremist northern Scottish isles, is a very diminutive animal... sometimes not more than seven hands and a half in height, and rarely exceeding nine and a half. He is often exceedingly beautiful, with a small head, good tempered countenance, a short*

Shetland foals are enchanting. Stelbar of Transy seen here with her mother, Stelstar of Transy.

neck, fine towards the throttle, shoulders low and thick,... in so little a creature far from being a blemish... back short, quarters expanded and powerful, legs flat and fine, and pretty round feet. These ponies possess immense strength for their size, will fatten upon almost anything; and are perfectly docile. One of them nine hands (three feet in height) carried a man of twelve stone, forty miles in one day. In the southern parts of the kingdom the Shetlanders have a very pleasing appearance harnessed to a light garden chair or carrying an almost baby rider. There are several of them now running in Windsor Park.

Gaining confidence on the lead rein.

A frontispiece to Boswell's *A Tour of the Hebrides with Dr Samuel Johnson* has a sketch of the doctor mounted on a small grey pony. The caption reads, 'Johnson on a Highland sheltie'. So it seems that on

their arrival in the islands the party changed from the mainland Highland ponies to the native small ponies.

The Shetland pony was used by the islanders as a pack pony, shepherd's pony and a means of transport. A number were sent to the mainland where they proved of great use as pack animals in the wilder and more remote areas of Scotland.

In 1874 when mine owners were banned from employing children to work in the coal mines, the stockier type of black male Shetlands took their place hauling coal. Some of these were crossed with native Welsh ponies to breed strong pit ponies.

In the Victorian age wealthy visiting Americans discovered the Shetland pony. They took the breed to their hearts and bought the ponies in great quantities, so much so that it is recorded that nearly all the 'pretty colours' were sent across the water. The Americans were willing to pay high prices for light-coloured ponies for their children to ride. For many years the base colour here has been black and brown, with the occasional bay, chestnut or grey. However, in the last decade more and more Shetlands of all colours have appeared in the show rings, no doubt descendants of the few light colours left unsold in the distant past.

When the native breeds were revived after World War II, the Shetland got a bad reputation as being too strong for children and not having an equable temperament. This was taken up by the cartoonist Thelwell, who produced hilarious books on children and ponies that depicted a Shetland-type animal in all manner of ludicrous situations.

The modern Shetland has had to earn the place that it now so rightly owns as the most excellent mount for the baby rider as well as for those of a slightly older age.

Characteristics of the Shetland

The Shetland does not exceed 10.5 hh (42in) and can be as small as 7 hh (28in).

mane, forelock and tail are long and thick and, although adding to the ponies' beauty, are really a protection against the worst weather. They should not be pulled or trimmed, only well brushed and tidied.

All colours are permitted, except spotted, and this is the only breed of native pony that allows the registration of piebald and skewbald.

Shetlands are free moving and have a fair

Left: from Mr Dougal Dick's famous and long-established Shetland stud, Rosallyn of Transy shows the type and style of the breed.
Below: Hose Elizabeth as a two-year-old.

Several studs now breed 'miniature' Shetlands. The present-day Shetland has a medium sized head, a rather dished face with a well shaped muzzle and a strong jaw capable of grazing poor growth. The ears are medium sized and the eyes large and kindly. A strong, well-shaped neck fits into good shoulders with a well developed chest. The body is deep and strong with well rounded quarters. The bone is in balance with the body and the pony has muscular forearms, short, strong cannons and large, flat knees. The round, pretty feet with strong horn are a feature of the breed. Many of these ponies are never shod.

In winter the ponies carry a thick, heavy and weather-resistant coat, which moults out over the spring months. The turn of speed for such small animals. Their temperaments must be equable, and the pony willing, biddable and forward going. Care must be taken in their initial breaking and schooling. It is better to work with the pony, rather than pitting one's will against a small animal which can be stubborn unless tactfully handled.

A matching pair of Shetland ponies makes an elegant turnout.

overawed, and when the inevitable tumble takes place, the ground is not so far away and the child is less frightened than by falling from a greater height.

Because of their great popularity, Shetlands have classes at most shows, the in-hand classes being particularly well filled. For people who want to come into natives but are not anxious to ride, the breed offers the opportunity for ownership of an interesting small animal with an intriguing history, and the chance to make friends with like-minded people.

Although some of the longest established and most famous Shetland studs are situated in Scotland, the ponies are now spread all over Britain. In the Shetland Isles the ponies still graze on the hillsides, providing much pleasure for the many visitors.

With its ability to survive and do well on rough-grazing, the Shetland does not need rich grass. This will cause it to put on too much weight which will be difficult to remove and may lead to laminitis. It is necessary to control the hours of grazing and to be careful of the type and amount of short feed given when the pony is in daily work.

The Shetland as a first pony for little children cannot be bettered. It is small enough so that the child does not feel

For small children the Shetland provides a good basic step to future enjoyment of riding and pony owning. As they grow, they find that the good-looking, well-schooled Shetland can take

The Shetland Pony Display Team stole the limelight at the National Pony Society's Centenary Show in 1993.

its place with the other mountain and moorland breeds and compete under saddle on equal terms. The small sections of the mountain and moorland ridden and Working Hunter Pony classes are open to it, it can go in leading rein, first ridden classes and gymkhanas, and appears thoroughly to enjoy dressing up for the Fancy Dress class.

Many successful horsemen and women had their first introduction to hounds and the hunting field from the back of a Shetland pony. For the adult, the Shetland is an excellent driving pony that singly, in pairs or teams of four, takes part with great success in driving events.

When the Shetland's fleetness of foot was brought to the notice of show organisers, the Shetland Pony Grand National was organised and is now one of the most popular events at many shows. The school-aged riders and their small mounts have to ride a course over small natural jumps. To compete in this event is the ambition of many young Shetland pony owners. The final takes place at The Horse of the Year Show.

Saddles can be of leather or felt, while for the first-time tiny rider it is still possible to obtain one of the old 'basket' saddles used in former times. Many Shetlands also need a crupper, that is, a loop of leather fastened to a metal eye on the back of the saddle. The tail is threaded through the leather loop which fits round the pony's dock and prevents the saddle from slipping forward. A crupper is essential if the pony has broad shoulders

A Shetland is everyone's best friend!

and the saddle 'rides up', thereby putting the young rider in the wrong position.

The Shetland Pony Stud Book Society, formed in 1890, is the oldest society of any of the native breeds. It takes care of all matters concerning the breed, including the registrations. Several sales exclusively confined to Shetlands are held during the year in the Shetland Isles, Scotland and England, and these are well attended by potential buyers not only from the United Kingdom but from many other countries. Attendance at one of the sales will give the potential Shetland owner a good insight into the breed but would-be owners are advised to take an experienced person with them if they intend to purchase a pony.

Chapter 7

The Efficient and Stylish Connemara

History of the breed

In 1565 Blunville wrote, *The Irish hobby, a pretty, fine horse having a good head. A pleasant ambler but also useful for men with darts and spears.* Another writer of the times comments that they were 'pretty ponies for ladies'.

In the past the smaller horses or ponies in Ireland were frequently known as 'hobbies', and no doubt this is where the name 'hobby-horse' originated for the child's toy.

The wild and rugged region of Connemara is noted for its mountains and boggy valleys, the heavy rainfall and the gales from the Atlantic that lash the region. As a result, the Connemara ponies are more than usually hardy.

The romantic theory is that native mares were covered by Andalusian stallions that swam ashore from ships of the Spanish Armada that had been wrecked on the rocks in the fierce storms. Other writers subscribe to the more mundane theory that the stallions were imported from Spain by those who

Elegance in action: Sydserff Golden Oak ridden by Barbara Gallimore.

Connemara ponies by the Sky Road, Clifden, Co. Galway. Photograph by Pat Lyne.

wanted to improve the indigenous breed. The outline and grace of the present-day Connemara pony points to there being more than a grain of truth in one of these stories.

With a breed so long established it is strange that all Youatt, writing in *The Horse*, can say is, *There is a native breed in Ulster, hardy and sure footed, but with little pretension to beauty and speed.* This follows a eulogy on the hunters and cavalry horses bred in Ireland in the 19th century, some of whom, if not all, probably had Connemara in their ancestry.

In the past the ponies carried peat in packs, worked on the small farms and pulled sledges to carry dung and forage. Later, they pulled small carts in which the farmer and his family could take produce to market. The more elegant of the breed found their way into the hands of the gentry where they were greatly prized as riding animals.

The Connemara can be counted as one of Ireland's most successful exports. Its strength allied to its beauty has commended it to pony enthusiasts from far and wide. Buyers from many countries attend the sales held regularly in Ireland.

Characteristics of the Connemara

The head of the Connemara pony should be short, slightly dished and with a deep cheekbone. It is wide between the eyes which should be full and dark. There is no coarseness about the muzzle, and the

small hacks. All colours are permissible except skewbald and piebald. The most popular colour appears to be grey, and there are a number of dun, bay and brown ponies and some chestnut and roan.

The 13 hh Connemara is slightly more rugged than its full-sized brother. Having such a kind nature, it is an ideal mount for school-aged children, especially those who like Hunter Trials, Working Hunter, jumping and hunting, for the Connemara at all heights is superb over fences, jumping cleanly and safely.

nostrils are large and open. Ears are small, nicely set and flexible. The neck is graceful, clean throated, slightly arched and set well into fine, sloping shoulders. A well-developed chest, giving a good forehand, is complemented by a deep, well-rounded barrel, strong back and loin and rounded, well-muscled quarters with well-set tail. The pony has strong forearms, short cannons, and very well-formed, round feet of hard horn. The breed is noted for well-shaped, hard feet and strong legs of good, flat bone. The overall outline and movement is of a pony with elegance allied with strength and scope. Biddable in temperament, Connemaras break well and school on calmly. On modern busy roads they prove quiet and sensible.

The height ranges from 13 hh to 14.2 hh. Connemara ponies going over height are often sold on to become successful

Above: a typical brood mare and noted winner, Pat Lyne's Chiltern Lara. Photograph by Carol Gilson. Top: the characteristic head of the breed as shown by Shipton Sea Image.

They are excellent Pony Club mounts, being immensely versatile and, while loving the speed and excitement of the gymkhana ring, are equally at home in riding classes. They are gentle enough for young owners to care for themselves, and

Shipton Sea Image displays the free movement so prized in the breed.

Ears pricked, well under control, but going eagerly – a true Connemara. Photograph by Shaw-Shot.

smaller family members will have a safe first introduction to riding from the back of their brother or sister's pony.

The Connemara is often chosen as a mount by adults who want an animal with stamina and elegance, but do not want the expense of a horse. The Connemara will suit them admirably as it can compete in all disciplines undertaken by horses.

There are plenty of in-hand and ridden classes for the breed, which can also go in mixed mountain and moorland classes. For those keen on riding club work or just as a hack, the Connemara will fill the bill. Often one Connemara of around 13.1–14 hh will meet the needs of several riders in one family. Apart from breed classes, Connemaras shine in open competition and many are successful in Show Hunter pony classes.

The breed is very successful in the show jumping arena and in junior eventing. In the hunting field the ponies are fast, stay well and jump safely.

All heights break satisfactorily to harness, giving a good looking, controlled, driving pony. They are excellent as ride and drive ponies.

After the Great Famine in the 19th century, the breed declined both in type and numbers. In 1923, the

Connemara Pony Breeders Society was founded in Galway with the object of conserving, developing and improving the breed. Inspections of the stock were undertaken and the best selected for entry into the first volume of the Stud Book which was published in 1926.

The English Connemara Pony Society was first formed in 1947 when the National Pony Society opened a register for the breed. The ECPS was re-constituted in 1953, and in 1979 undertook the production and printing of the Stud Book. It appoints representatives in various regions who assist members, organise functions and monitor the welfare of Connemaras around the country. The Society maintains a list of ponies for sale, and publishes *The Connemara Chronicle*, a most interesting and informative Year Book.

Enthusiastically going cross country.
Photograph by Pleasure Prints.

Chapter 8

The Versatile and Useful New Forest Pony

History of the breed

At one time, the New Forest covered nearly 600,000 acres and extended from the Avon to Southampton and as far north as Wiltshire. Ponies have been running on the Forest for many centuries and are among the local animals mentioned in a document dating from the reign of King Canute. In the 11th century the Forest was a royal hunting ground for William the Conqueror and in King John's time there was a Royal Stud at Brockenhurst, the yearly profits going towards the costs of building Beaulieu Abbey.

King Henry VIII, no doubt because his own great bulk required a large animal, decreed that all equines under the height of 14 hh be slaughtered, but one can be fairly certain that those then referred to as 'the little dark denizens of the Forest' hid some of the smaller ponies away until happier times.

The blood of many breeds runs in the veins of the New Forest pony. In the mid-

The Boxing Day point-to-point over the Forest is one of the highlights of the year. Miss P V Mangin wins the Veteran Riders' Class on Busy Lizzie.

18th century the thoroughbred 'Marske', the sire of the great racehorse 'Eclipse', served a number of Forest mares. Youatt (1859) says, *Old Marske, before his value was known, contributed to the Hampshire breed. The modern New Foresters, not withstanding their Marske blood, are generally ill made, large headed, short necked and ragged hipped; but hardy, safe and useful with much of their ancient spirit and speed, and all their old paces.*

In the mid 19th century Prince Albert lent the Arab stallion 'Zorah' who stood at New Park, but the commoners who owned the mares did not wish to bring them from their haunts, and consequently 'Zorah' was not much used.

In 1918 the winning polo pony stallion 'Field Marshall' stood at stud and later the Dales-bred 'Weardale Hero' was also used. At different times other breeds have been turned out on the Forest, among them Welsh, Exmoor and Highland and, in the last century, even a Basuto pony. From this jumble emerged a recognisable type, hardy, strong and durable.

In the past many ponies were used on the Forest holdings for pulling small ploughs, drawing carts or dragging timber. They were saddle animals for the family, and also used for carting deer.

The affairs of the Forest are administered by a Court of Verderers that appoints Agisters to patrol the Forest and attend to the needs of the animals turned out by the commoners who have rights of grazing.

The many ponies running the Forest have to compete with cattle and donkeys

Wootton Firedance demonstrates the suitability of the breed for harness work.

New Forest ponies and their riders race for the winning post at the Boxing Day point-to-point.

for the available forage. The New Forest has suffered erosion of habitat due to the expansion of the road systems and the large tracts of land taken for car and caravan parks and camping areas.

The Forest roads were fenced off some years ago, and many small side roads closed. To reach their haunts or watering places the ponies now have to take the underpasses made for them. Before fencing, ponies could be found in all the villages and towns and grazing on the sides of the road round Ringwood and up as far as Downton and beyond. They also grazed down all the lanes around the Christchurch area, earning the name of 'lane creepers'. This access to extra grazing ended when the fences were erected. The pony, like the other semi-feral grazers, finds itself marginalised to make way for road building, house construction and the needs of the tourist.

In spite of main roads being fenced off and a 40 mph speed limit imposed on every Forest road, there is still a heavy toll of casualties among the pony population every year. All this poses constant problems for both Verderers and Agisters, as well as the commoners themselves. For the tourists who descend on it in their thousands, much of the charm of the Forest lies in the presence of the ponies. Little do the visitors realise that their constant demands for more facilities endanger the very attraction they have come to see.

Characteristics of the New Forest

Until the end of World War II, the maximum height of the New Forest pony was 14 hh but, because of the demand for larger ponies, it was raised to 14.2 hh. The breed now has the widest range of heights of any of the native breeds, from 11.2 hh to 14.2 hh, making it one of the most versatile and useful ponies for a family.

Sturdily built and without any exaggerations, the New Forest pony stands on well-boned legs with short, strong cannons and good joints. The feet should be of a size appropriate for the height of the animal, never upright in pastern nor down at the heel, nor yet a donkey shape, but round with good depth of strong horn. Forest ponies are very agile and active, and in their homeland have to traverse some rough and often boggy places, so good feet are very important. The pony should have a clean cut head with a good-sized, intelligent eye. It should not be over-long from eye to muzzle tip, and the ears should be of moderate size. The neck should have some elegance, and fit comfortably into well-laid 'riding' shoulders, giving a good length of rein. It is deep through the heart and strong in back and loin with well-rounded quarters. The tail should be well set but not over-high and never drooping. Both tail and mane should be of good quality hair with a bright sheen. Mane and tail may be pulled and trimmed and heels trimmed for shows.

Plaits and braids are not allowed in classes confined to native breeds, but the New Forest may be plaited for other classes. All colours except piebald, skewbald and blue-eyed creams are permissible but, since 1992, no dark-eyed, very light chestnut, pale palomino or creams have been accepted except as mares and geldings. Most New Forest ponies break well and easily, but if a novice buys an unbroken pony it is advisable to find an experienced person to do the breaking and initial schooling, as inexpert handling in the early stages has ruined many a good animal for life.

The New Forest is a very friendly and co-operative pony, loves human company and trains easily for the various tasks the

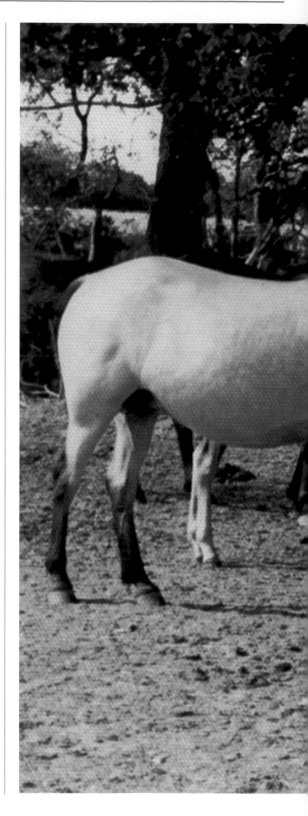

The Knightwood Stud has a long-established line of dun New Forest ponies.

They make excellent hunting ponies, especially in their own habitat where they instinctively take the safest route to avoid bogs and the worst ground.

New Forest ponies tend to put on extra weight easily, and care must be taken not to let a pony get too fat. They thrive well on good, but not rich, grazing, but during spring and autumn flushes when the new grass grows quickly they should be brought in for some

owner wishes it to perform. Because of its equable temperament it is well fitted as a pony for children and young people, and it looks after the more nervous and unsure. Many are used with great success by the Riding for Disabled Association, and yet perform prodigious feats for the ambitious rider.

As long as they are well boned and have sound joints, New Forest ponies can be exercised by the adults of the family. Those in the 14.2 hh height range can carry quite a bit of weight.

The smaller ponies are ideal for young children, being kindly and sensible, good on the roads and safe enough for their small riders to help with the catching, grooming and feeding. With older children, the New Forest pony enjoys almost any equine enterprise. The larger pony makes a good ride for adults; many have taken well to show jumping and they are sure footed and fast in Hunter Trials.

Above: competing in Working Hunter Pony Class.

Top: Merrie Marmalade, a New Forest stallion.

hours out of each 24 to lessen the risk of laminitis. Good quality hay and a balanced ration of short feed are necessary for ponies in work.

All ponies bred on the Forest carry a brand, which is registered in the owner's name by the breed's Society. Round-ups are held each year when the branding takes place. New Forest ponies from registered parents may be registered with the Society and appear in the Stud Book, so the pony can be traced back to its breeder for the whole of its life. New Forest ponies without papers, although well bred, cannot be registered or compete in breed classes where the registration number has to be given.

The ponies on the Forest are rounded up, or 'drifted', at various times of the year so that they can be identified by their owners. Some are returned to the Forest, others taken back to the holdings for the owners' use or sent to the Beaulieu Road Pony Sales which take place regularly.

In 1901, in an endeavour to improve the stock on the Forest, the Society for the Improvement of New Forest Ponies was formed with the aim of holding a stallion show at which premiums were awarded. The first show for mares and foals was held in 1905 and, as a result, the Burley and District New Forest Pony and Cattle Society was formed and the Stud Book started. In 1938, both societies merged to form the New Forest Pony and Cattle Breeding Society which has administered the affairs of the breed since that date. There is also a New Forest Pony Enthusiasts' Club.

Until recently, the annual show and races were held on August Bank Holiday in Burley Park. Although still on the same day, the show has now moved to New Park, Brockenhurst while the races are held separately near Lyndhurst. The Stallion Show, once held in the spring, is also at New Park on the Saturday before the annual show. An exciting three mile Point-to-Point is held over the Forest every Boxing Day. There is an enthusiastic and thriving driving community in Hampshire and Dorset and many ponies are broken to harness and take part in drives and rallies over the Forest. They compete with success in driving classes at shows up and down the country.

Many of the big agricultural shows and all the larger pony shows put on in-hand and ridden classes for the breed, and they are eligible for all mixed native classes.

Fury, owned by Mr J Adams, runs out all year on the Forest and is brought in to compete at the annual Stallion Show.

Chapter 9

The Attractive and Adaptable Fell

History of the breed

It is generally understood that the Fell and Dales breeds are descended from the Galloways, which for many centuries served the far north of England and the Scottish borders with useful hardy pack and riding ponies.

The Galloway was described by Youatt as: *bright bay or brown, between 13 hh to 14 hh with small head and neck, and peculiarly deep, clean legs. Its qualities were speed, stoutness and sure footedness over a very rugged and mountainous country.*

The Galloways were bred from the ponies already in Britain crossed, it is believed, with other breeds brought to this country from abroad. Notable among these are the Friesian stallions that accompanied the Roman Legions who came to patrol Hadrian's Wall.

The Fell has a fascinating and romantic history. It is still bred in numbers in the north-west of Britain where some of the most famous studs are located, but its fame has spread beyond its native counties and it can now be found all over the United Kingdom.

Fell pony brood mares and foals in their native Cumbria.

Old records going back to the 15th century tell of the pack ponies working out of Kendal. In strings of 20 or more they were led by the 'bell mare' who wore a collar of bells round her neck to warn other users of the track that the pack train was coming and to move out of the way. Pack ponies transported wool and cloth from the north to Southampton and returned with loads of figs, raisins, dyes and other goods to be sold by the merchants of Cumberland and Westmoreland.

Pony racing became a great sport in the area during the 19th century.

Characteristics of the Fell

The Fell pony does not exceed 14 hh. It is strongly built for its size but without lumber, and is very active and forward going.

The head is well-shaped, with large eyes, small ears and good open nostrils. The expression is calm and friendly. The mane and tail are profuse and of good quality hair, which should be kept well

Mr Jim Bell's Waverhead Pearl, champion Fell at the Royal Show. Photograph by Roy Wallis.

The Fell ponies also worked all over the north carrying coal, wool and butter. Some, nearer the coast, were no doubt used by wreckers and smugglers to transport contraband. They were notable pack animals before the road system was advanced and wheeled vehicles finally took over, when they became excellent driving ponies.

brushed but not trimmed. The profuse forelock covers the forehead often to just above the nostrils. With its good length of neck, this covering gives the Fell an aristocratic appearance.

In winter the Fell grows a deep, weatherproof coat which it throws off in spring to display a shining covering that

Fells make smart driving ponies. Bewcastle Bouquet to a Mills Gig. Photograph by Charles Donaldson.

excels with good grooming. The legs behind and below the hock and round the hoof should display good feathering which must not be trimmed off, but kept clean and well brushed. This hair, except that at the point of the heel, tends to be cast off in summer.

The barrel is deep and well rounded, with a good strong back and loin and large, rounded quarters. The pony has strong flat bone, muscular forearms, short cannons and well shaped, hard feet.

The long, easy stride at the walk is an inheritance from the Fell's pack pony forebears while the smart, ground-covering trot harks back to when the breed took to the shafts and trotting matches were a favourite sport in the north. 'A good walker is a good galloper', the saying goes, and these ponies can be amazingly fast when requested.

The Fell is hardy and strong, and thrives on natural and rough grazing. Too much lush grass will lead to obesity and the problems which accompany this state.

Marlingdyke Millstream comes home fresh from an endurance ride. Photograph by Eric Jones.

Clive Richardson's Border Black Empress going well in Junior Showjumping...

As a breed, the Fell has a calm, biddable nature and becomes a great family friend, responding readily to affection from humans. Black is the most common colour, with some brown, bay and grey. As many Fells are still bred in their native area, they have retained their health, strength and hardiness.

The breed will appeal to those who like long distance riding and treks over wild landscapes, for this pony is both comfortable and sure footed.

Nowadays the Fell pony can be found taking part in every sort of competition, as well as being shown in breed classes, in-hand and under saddle. It competes in large mixed mountain and moorland classes, and shines as a working hunter, jumping swiftly and cleanly yet showing great control. The Fell is excellent across country.

The Fell pony is ideal for a family as it is kind enough for the young ones, adventurous enough for the teenagers and strong enough for the adults, the latter finding it a most useful animal for all Riding Club activities. The breed has also been used extensively for Riding and Driving for the Disabled. In driving they shine brightly. Queen Elizabeth II has a stud of Fell ponies, and teams are frequently driven in cross-country competition by HRH Prince Philip. Often ridden to hounds, the Fell proves a good stayer in all going, and is a reliable hack for the non-competitive rider. Many people who started riding as children on Exmoor or Dartmoor ponies find that the Fell pony is a natural progression as they grow.

Although the first meeting to form the Fell Pony Society was held in 1916, World War I delayed its formation until 1918, since when it has conducted all the affairs of the breed.

Until 1980 all Fell ponies were registered with the National Pony Society, but in that year the Fell Pony Society decided to publish its own Stud Book, and the first issue came out in 1981.

Each year the Society holds a Breed show, a Stallion and Colt show and spring performance trials, while there is now a Southern Fell Pony Show to accommodate the large number of the breed in the southern half of the United Kingdom.

... and showing her versatility by carrying her owner in an adult competition. Photograph by Carol Gilson.

Characteristics of the Dales

A Dales pony has a height limit of 14.2 hh. It has powerful and well-laid shoulders with a good chest. The body is short-coupled with strong loins and well-developed ribs. The neck is muscular and of ample length, and the withers are not too fine. The quarters are broad and well rounded with muscular thighs and strong hocks. The ponies have neat heads showing no dish, and are broad between

The action of the Dales sets the seal on the breed. It is straight and true with great use of knees and hocks giving powerful drive. The mane, forelock and tail are long and flowing, and there should be silky hair round the foot and on the heel. Of great courage and stamina, the Dales combines these attributes with intelligence, a calm temperament and an iron constitution. The colour is mostly black, with some bay, brown and grey and,

Mrs V James' Abdylane Nancy displays the outline and construction of the Dales. Note the coloured ribbons plaited in the top of the tail, seen only on Dales. Photograph by Anthony Reynolds.

the eyes, which should be large, dark and kindly. The muzzle is relatively small, there is no coarseness about the jaw, and the breed has incurving pony ears. The forearms are short and muscular, cannons short and strong with 20–22.5cm (8–9in) of flinty bone, and the pasterns are flexible and of good length. The Dales is renowned for its large, hard, well-shaped feet.

occasionally, roan. The Dales is a hardy survivor, and comparatively easy for a new owner to look after. Grazing must not be too lush and, for those in work, a well-thought-out programme of short feed is necessary.

With its kind temperament the Dales fits in well with a family. It is too big for small children, although the taller teenager can have unlimited fun with one.

This herd, owned by Mr F Bruce, lives out all year. Note the thick winter coats.

The adult rider who enjoys hunting and riding across country will find a Dales pony very suitable.

For those interested in the driving scene, a Dales fits the bill nicely. With its outward appearance and inner strength combined with its durability and fast, eye-catching action, it is successful at driving events and shows all over Britain. There are classes for the breed at many of the bigger shows, and it is able to compete in any of the large mixed mountain and moorland classes, showing in-hand or under saddle and Working Hunter Pony.

The Dales is a willing and clever jumper, and enjoys cross country events and Hunter Trials. For those more interested in social riding than competition, the Dales is just as good for hacking, long distance riding and trekking.

The Dales and Fell breeds started separate breed societies in 1917. Dales were registered and appeared in the stud book of the National Pony Society until 1981 after which the Dales Pony Society published its own Stud Book. Dales ponies with three generations of recorded breeding on both sides are eligible for registration. The Society also registers and licenses all approved Dales stallions. The Society runs spring and summer breed shows, a breed performance show, an annual pleasure ride and a Dales pony driving rally.

For the novice adult and, in particular, the well-built rider who wants a friend as well as a trustworthy ride, the Dales pony is hard to beat.

The Dales is a stylish jumper, as shown by Mr A Reeves' Eskrigg Donna. Photograph by Anthony Reynolds.

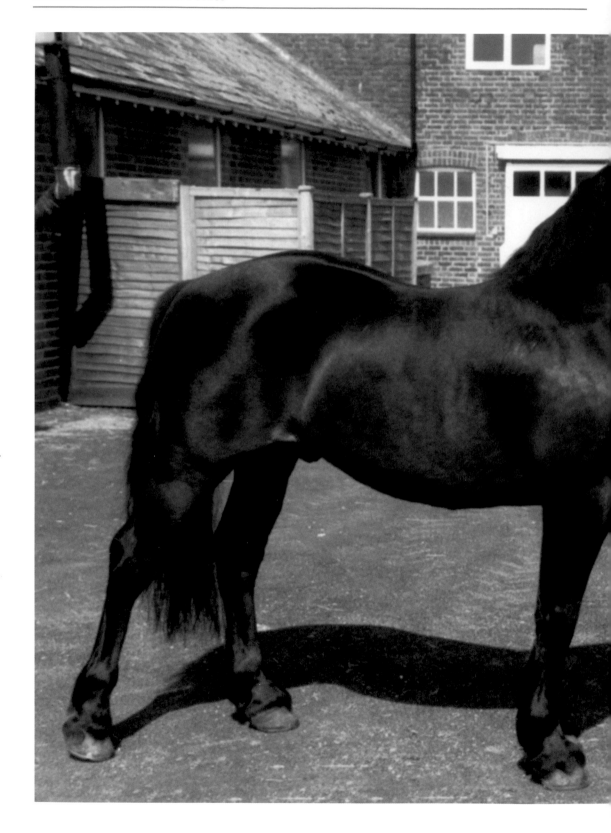

Chapter 11

Welsh Ponies and Cobs

There are four sections in the Stud Book of the Welsh Pony and Cob Society and these bring the number of our native breeds to twelve. The sections are as follows:

Section A: Welsh Mountain ponies not to exceed 12 hh.

Section B: Welsh ponies not to exceed 13.2 hh.

Section C: Welsh ponies (Cob type) not to exceed 13.2 hh.

Section D: Welsh Cobs over 13.2 hh.

The ponies in all four sections have the same basic make, shape and characteristics and differ only in size. All colours, except piebald and skewbald, are allowed.

SECTION A: The charismatic Welsh Mountain pony

Youatt writing in *The Horse* (1859) said, *The Welsh pony is one of the most beautiful little animals that can be imagined. He has a*

Welsh Cob Section D Stallion, Llanarth Welsh Warrior, owned by Mrs P Vestey.

Welsh Section A ponies on the mountain. Photograph by Wynne Davies.

small head, high withers, deep yet round barrel, short joints, flat legs and good round feet. He will live on any fare and never tire.

In those days pony hunting was a favourite pastime with Welsh farmers, who pursued herds of mountain ponies on horseback and with dogs and, using lassos with great skill, captured the best of the little animals. The ponies were sold at markets such as Bala, where the sum of £4 or £5 per pony was a good price for the hill farmers who always had a hard time making a living.

The Welsh Mountain pony is still renowned for its beautiful head and this, coupled with its proportions of body and limbs and breath-taking movement, makes it perhaps the most charismatic of the native breeds.

To see the breed in the ring today, so well bred and cared for, it is easy to forget that Welsh Mountain ponies owe their existence to the hardiness and gritty determination of their ancestors to survive on the inhospitable mountains. It was once written that they were 'little animals who can survive where sheep and cattle die', and were 'the living personification of the survival of the fittest, every instinct sharpened by self-preservation and every limb tested by exertion'.

This is another breed where the romantics believe that the indigenous stock was infused with the blood of Arab stallions swimming ashore from wrecks on the Welsh coast. This may or may not be true, but there is Arab blood in the breed which several breeders introduced in the 19th century 'to glamorise the breed'. (One of these well-meaning breeders was Richard Crawshay Bailey, a distant relative of mine.)

The most usual colours of Welsh Mountain ponies in the past centuries were bay, black and brown, with a proportion of chestnuts, a few duns, creams and roans, and a handful of greys. All that changed with the advent of 'Dyoll Starlight', who was foaled in 1894 and lived to be 31 years old. He stood 11.2hh and revolutionised the breed. He is still spoken of with reverence wherever Welsh Mountain ponies are discussed. 'Dyoll Starlight' was a grey stallion and this colour has dominated the breed since his day.

Like all the native breeds, the Welsh suffered deprivations during the two World Wars, but the numbers have increased rapidly since 1950.

Welsh Mountain pony stallion Traefae's Taran, photographed by Wynne Davies.

Characteristics of the Welsh Mountain

To look at, the Welsh Mountain pony is a study in beauty and symmetry. It has a small head with neat, pointed ears and a wide forehead between eyes that are large and bold and sparkling with life. A clean-cut jaw tapers to a small muzzle. In profile the head should be slightly dished but never straight or convex. The neck is clean and of good length, well carried and set strongly into sloping shoulders with a well-defined wither and good chest.

Limbs are set square, with strong forearms, short cannons with good dense bone, and round dense hooves. The tail is set high and well carried. The mane, forelock and tail are flowing and of good quality hair. The action is spectacular with

great power in the quarters and flexion of the hocks and free use of the shoulders. The pony must be straight both in front and behind, quick, free and rhythmic, and in profile can best be described as 'poetry in motion'.

country and junior one-day events. For younger children they are safe and suitable rides for Nursery and Cradle Stakes, and for all Pony Club activities. One of their greatest successes in recent years has been as mounts for young riders

The Welsh Mountain is a most elegant and suitable leading rein pony. Wharley Rosebud ridden by Lucy Cook. Photograph by Pleasure Prints.

Kindly in nature, well built and small, the Welsh Mountain makes the ideal child's pony, and can be used for very small children for first time riding lessons. In the show ring they are very successful in lead rein and first ridden classes. With older children they compete in breed and mixed mountain and moorland classes with great success.

Quick, clean, willing and safe jumpers, they excel in Working Hunter Pony, cross

in the Prince Philip Games for, with their strength, speed and agility, they can quickly out-manoeuvre and out-distance the opposition.

Being hardy and strong, the Welsh Mountain pony can live and thrive on good but not rich grass. However, it needs some short feed and hay in winter and when in regular work. It does put on weight easily, so care in management is advised.

SECTION B: The popular Welsh pony

With the same true Welsh characteristics, the Welsh pony excelled in bone and feet and had great stamina. It was the hill farmer's pony, the main means of transport for the people in the isolated holdings on the mountains and in the valleys. Used for rounding up sheep and driving the pony herds, for work on the holdings and for riding and driving, it was the mainstay of the remote districts.

The stallion 'Tan-y-Bwlch Berwyn' is regarded as the pioneer stud of the modern Welsh Section B. He was by the Arab stallion 'Sahara', and was responsible for refining the breed over the years from a useful working pony to an elegant

Above: Mrs Johns-Powell's lovely Welsh B mare, Cottrell Aurora, photographed by Anthony Reynolds.
Top: Typical of a top-class Section B, Mrs Kofteros' Glansevin Gay Gordon.

ride for many young people, especially those anxious to compete in the show ring. The Section B with its pretty head, clean lines and flowing movement is very successful against all breeds of ponies.

Characteristics of the Welsh

The general description of the Welsh Mountain applies to the Welsh B, with a greater emphasis being placed on the riding pony qualities while retaining bone and remaining true to the Welsh type.

For school-aged children it is useful in many spheres as well as showing, as it is a bold and willing jumper, fast across country and makes a good hunter or junior eventer. Jumping, Working Pony and Show Hunter Pony classes all come within its capabilities. Many Welsh ponies have proved excellent gymkhana ponies,

joining the Welsh Mountain in Pony Club teams.

SECTION C: The functional Welsh pony of Cob type

This is one of the most useful of the Welsh breeds, as it is equally suitable for young people and adults. It has a true Welsh pony head with large, intelligent eyes, a strong but well-shaped neck cleanly fitted into well-laid shoulders giving a good length of rein. It is well built with strong bone but in no way coarse, and has the free and active movement of all its race.

It has an amiable disposition and soon becomes a loved and trusted family friend. It is a true dual-purpose animal, as it can compete in any discipline and especially shines in ride and drive or

A grand sight in harness, Gwelfro Tywysog, a Section C stallion.

Section C Waxwing Reward, photographed by Wynne Davies.

private driving, where its good build and carriage and spectacular movement put it at the top of many a line up. A scopey and forward-going jumper, it is excellent for hunting and cross country work.

SECTION D: The spectacular and capable Welsh Cob

The largest of the four Welsh breeds, the Cob inspires almost a reverence amongst its admirers. The keeping and breeding of Cobs in the Welsh valleys can be said to be almost as much a religion as a business!

The history of the Welsh Cob goes back into the mists of time. Some people believe that this was the mount of the knights in armour, and history records that they rode a breed of horse called a 'Rouncy'. The Rouncy of Powys was the most sought after of all mounts. In the 12th century an archbishop of Brecon recorded that the brave Welsh princes and chieftains rode 'swift and generous steeds' into battle.

Dr Wynne Davies, the highly-respected historian of the Welsh breeds, states that there are four dominant stallions, all of which feature in today's Cob pedigrees. One, 'Cymro Llwyd', foaled in the 1850s, was out of a fast-trotting mare owned by my great-great grandfather, William Crawshay.

Always admired for its size, strength and spectacular action, the Welsh Cob was described long ago as *having the outlook and poise of a stag, nostrils wide open like the barrel of a gun, the eyes like two ripe plums and dancing in the head, ears small and fine and restless like two sage leaves, and a coat like new silk.* The same description could be used for the breed today, so little has it altered.

In the 19th century a writer declared that the Welsh Cob was 'strong enough for the farm, swift enough to fetch the doctor in an emergency, handy enough to put to the cannon, and good enough for the cavalry to ride.'

limit for the Welsh Section D, so owners can decide for themselves which classes to enter according to the height of their ponies. The Welsh Cob is eligible to compete in all open ridden classes that apply only to native ponies.

The Welsh Cob's biddable nature, strength and stamina make it highly suitable as a hack, long distance ride or trekking pony.

Over the years the Welsh Cob has been renowned as a driving animal. Many well-known firms used these handsome and

Welsh Cob stallion Llanarth Welsh Warrior, Kentchurch Cerys and her foal, Kentchurch Challenger.

Characteristics of the Welsh Cob

The Welsh Cob has much to recommend it for the adult or tall teenager who wants a comfortable and athletic mount. It is a useful hunter and powerful jumper, safe and fast across country. It excels in working hunter pony classes, and animals over 14.2 hh are able to go in working hunter and Cob classes. There is no height

fast-moving ponies to move their goods around, and and they were a favourite to draw coaches and carriages. Today they feature with great success in driving competitions both across country and in the ring.

Enjoying an event. Photograph by Sue Feast.

Conclusion

For the family who owns a mare in any of these four sections who finds that her original use has disappeared, the idea of breeding a foal may appeal. Both Welsh Mountain and Section B pony can be bred to their own stallions, but both have bred notable riding ponies when put to a thoroughbred pony stallion. The Cobs Cob Society registers the ponies and cobs, keeps the Stud Book and administers to the needs of the breed in general. There is a great deal of activity in the Welsh breeds, with area societies and shows and sales up and down the country. All shows classify one or more of the Welsh sections, and they can take part in all mountain and moorland classes.

Kentchurch Commandant going fluently across country.

cross well with the thoroughbred horse, breeding show jumpers, hunting and event horses. Before starting to breed, however, it is necessary to take expert advice.

Founded in 1901, the Welsh Pony and Buyers come from all around the world to attend the sales, notably the Fayre Oaks Sale in the autumn, and very high prices are paid for the best of the ponies and cobs on offer. The reputation of the Welsh Cob is hard to beat!

Above: A couple in perfect accord with each other. Photograph by Anthony Reynolds.
Below: Welsh Cobs take pleasure in any discipline. Photograph by Pleasure Prints.

Chapter 12

Choosing the Right Breed

With such a wide variety of mountain and moorland breeds to choose from, there is indeed something for everyone. Before making your choice, decide what you want in a pony – size, shape and temperament.

To get a good idea of the breeds, go to one of the bigger agricultural shows such as the Royal Show at Stoneleigh or the Bath and West. You can take in either or both of the big pony shows: the National Pony Society show held at Malvern in early August, and the Ponies Association UK show which is held in the middle of August at Peterborough.

At these events you will see all breeds of native pony on display, in-hand, under saddle, jumping and in harness. Take a long look at all of them, see how they perform, what size and shape they are and try to decide which would fit in best with your own or your family's needs. You may fall in love with one particular breed immediately, but it may not be just the right one.

If you ride or are learning to ride, or have school-age children who may want

The Connemara is suitable for an adult or a teenager. Photograph by Shaw-Shot.

to ride, then a breed that can carry both adult and young person is the one to choose. If you are buying a pony for smaller children, your choice must fall on one of the smaller breeds. For the adult who wants only a good hack and possibly something to take to the local riding club or to go hunting then one of the heavier breeds might be just the thing.

Consider your requirements well when looking at performers in the mountain and moorland ridden classes. Are you tall or short? Slim or carrying a little weight? Youthful or not as young as of yore? Are you strong and capable or not so robust and a little timid?

Choose a breed that is up to your weight. Do not over-horse yourself if you are small and slim and not very strong, or under-horse if you are of larger stature. Some of the smaller natives, such as the Exmoor, can carry quite a bit of weight, but you

The Welsh D suits a tall, strong rider. Photograph by Anthony Reynolds.

are going to look a bit silly on top if you have long legs! Perhaps a Fell would suit you better. If you are slim and elegant consider the Connemara; if you are tall and strong the Welsh Section D Cob might well be your animal. There is indeed something for everyone among the mountain and moorland ponies.

Once you have chosen your breed, then find out all you can about it. Join the society that caters for the breed. Most big shows have a breed stand where you can

The small size New Forest makes an excellent lead rein pony. Photograph by Anthony Reynolds.

The Welsh Section B is an eager jumper. Baledon Commanchero ridden by Wendy Evans. Photograph by Mike Gash.

go to talk about the breed and collect useful literature.

Breeders of native ponies do not always have much spare time but they are always willing to give up an hour or two to people really anxious to see and learn about the ponies and be possible purchasers. Try to visit several studs of the breed that you think might suit you. Seeing the ponies at close hand and discussing them with their breeders may convince you that you have chosen aright.

Several sections of the equine press carry advertisements offering ponies of all sorts for sale and, although some are undoubtedly good buys, some that sound tempting may not be all they are cracked up to be. There are also many horse and pony sales held up and down the country where the entry is sold by auction, but I do not advise inexperienced would-be purchasers to buy their first pony at such a sale unless accompanied by an experienced and reliable person.

The best advice I can give to potential owners is to consult the sales list put out by the Society that caters for their chosen breed. All breed societies now maintain sales lists on which their members place the names and details of ponies they have for sale, and this often provides the very pony you have in mind. It is as well to have the pony vetted before buying it; this is not cheap but is worth paying for as, if the job is done correctly, it will at least ensure that you have an animal sound in wind and limb. You should be as particular about your pony's age, condition and habits as you are when purchasing a car.

I hope that the descriptions and photographs in this book have given you an idea of the breeds and their capabilities. To sum up, here is a guide of all 12, and the age and size of person suitable for each breed. This is given only for guidance, as all the native breeds are biddable and willing. Much depends on the age, height, weight and experience of the rider.

Adults under 5ft 2in may find their requirements adequately suited by one of the smaller breeds such as Exmoor, Dartmoor or Welsh Section B. The timid rider will find comfort and security on a pony such as the Fell or Highland; the sporting rider will enjoy the New Forest or Connemara, while the more adventurous and stronger rider will get excitement and

Whatever you want to do ...

pleasure from a Welsh Cob or Dales. I cannot emphasise too strongly that to gain full pleasure and satisfaction from owning and riding a native pony you and your mount should be compatible in all things.

Lead rein for smaller children:
Welsh Section A; Dartmoor; New Forest; Shetland.

First ride for small children:
Shetland; Welsh Sections A and B; Dartmoor; Exmoor; New Forest.

Hacking, hunting, cross country for adults and older teenagers:
Welsh Sections C and D; Connemara; New Forest; Fell; Dales; Highland.

Hacking, hunting, cross country, for children and young teenagers:
Welsh Sections A, B and C; Dartmoor; Exmoor; New Forest; Connemara; Fell.

Gymkhana:
Welsh A and B; New Forest; Dartmoor; Connemara; Shetland.

Working hunter and jumping for adults and older teenagers:
Welsh C and D; Connemara; New Forest; Fell; Dales; Highland.

Working hunter and jumping for children and younger teenagers:
Welsh A, B and C; Dartmoor; Exmoor; New Forest; Connemara; Shetland.

Hacking and/or hunting: all breeds.

Driving: all breeds.

...the native pony will oblige. Photograph by Clive Richardson.

Chapter 13

Cost of the Pony and Maintenance

It is not only young people or those with families who become first-time owners of ponies. Many people who have always longed for their own horse or pony have to wait until middle age before they can afford to purchase one, or have the time, means and place to keep one. However, it is unwise for anyone to buy a pony before they have thoroughly costed out what it will entail, not only in outlay for the animal but for tack, clothing, accommodation and maintenance.

Buying the pony

The first big outlay comes with the purchase of the pony itself. It would be unwise of me to name a figure, although I would suggest that you consider spending in the region of £800–£1000. If you are an experienced rider and wish to compete at a good level, then the cost of purchase will be much higher for the animal you want.

If you want the animal for immediate use, it is a waste of time and money to buy a youngster, who will need to be three years old before it can be broken, and four years before it can go in regular work. If you are a novice rider/owner, the youngster would need to go to an experienced person for breaking and initial schooling, and then probably you would need to engage the services of a good rider to complete the schooling. All this is very expensive. I have watched people at native pony sales letting their hearts rule their heads and out of pity buying a weak, thin foal or a wretched screw of a youngster. Neither will do anything for them but cost a great deal of money and give endless heartache and disappointment.

For the first-time buyer who wants to ride, it is better to purchase a pony of six years or older that has been well-broken, preferably used by a family, is kind and quiet and, above all, is safe on the road. The most important thing to remember when purchasing any animal is manners. Ponies that do misbehave, bolt, rear, jib, buck, or that are nappy, morose, sullen, too highly strung or unsafe in traffic, are not suitable for novice owners. Good manners put extra on the price, but they are well worth paying for.

Stabling

There are several options for stabling a pony if you have no facilities yourself, but they are all relatively expensive.

The first is to keep the pony at full livery at a reliable yard. The cost should cover everything except transport, veterinary bills, shoeing and insurance, all of which will be extra.

The second is half livery, where the pony will be housed and fed. Sometimes mucking out is included in the cost and sometimes the owner is expected to take turns with this essential duty. The owner is responsible for grooming, exercising, and so on.

A clean, well-cared for stable block is a real joy.

Enjoying a hose down on a warm summer's day.

The third is do-it-yourself livery where you pay for the hire of a loosebox and grazing. It is up to you to supply all the short feed, hay and so on, and go twice daily to do all the work and keep the pony exercised.

There are a great many yards in Britain offering such facilities. It is an ideal way of keeping a pony, especially for the older first-time pony owner who has never had to do hard manual labour outside in all weathers, or for families who would find it difficult to look after the pony full-time.

It is essential to visit a number of yards in your area, find out the charges and also to talk to people who know the yards and can recommend one suitable for your needs. It will be easy to judge which are the most efficient yards. The stabling will be well built and maintained, and doors strong and properly secured. The yard itself should be clean with no loose straw blowing about, the muck heap well built, and all implements put away. The paddocks where the ponies graze should be free of weeds, strongly fenced and with good gates and a fresh water supply. Stables should be well bedded down and any horses and ponies in should look clean, well groomed and content. The staff should be pleasant and helpful. Watch the way they approach the animals and the animals' reactions; by this you can judge whether the handling is good. Paperwork should be presented in an efficient and businesslike manner.

When you settle on a yard and book in your pony, it is advisable to have a contract stating what you expect for your money. Also find out what the stables require; for example, some would expect to use your pony when you are not riding it. If you are agreeable, stipulate in the contract how many hours and on which days in a week the pony may be used by the proprietors. If you prefer the pony to be kept strictly for your own use or for people nominated by you, this should be in the contract.

Insurance

It goes without saying that you should take out a comprehensive insurance policy on the pony to cover you in case of robbery, accident, illness or death, and most policies offer help with veterinary fees. Charges can be quite high, so shop around the various insurance companies that offer horse and pony cover before making up your mind. Do read the policy carefully, particularly the claims part, so you are sure how and when a claim should be made. Failure to do this may find your claim disallowed on some minor technical point, such as the length of time after the loss, accident or onset of illness that the claim had to be received by the insurers.

Keeping your pony at home

If you intend to keep the pony on your own premises, be sure you own enough grazing or can hire grazing locally in fields or paddocks. Avoid orchards in autumn as the ponies may annoy the owners by picking the apples off the lower branches. There is also the possibility of the ponies choking on the apples or gobbling up windfalls and getting colic. Avoid fields that have yew trees growing in the hedges, as this tree is highly poisonous.

If the field has no large trees to act as a break against bad weather or shade from the sun, it is wise to construct an open-fronted shelter situated with its back to the prevailing wind. Although few native ponies take advantage of shelter in cold weather they do like to get out of the sun and flies in hot spells. Not less than two to three acres of grazing should be available, more if more than one pony is to be kept, as some pasture must always be shut up to recover while the other part is grazed.

A good water supply in a proper water trough is essential. In these days ponies should not have to rely on a pond or stream that could become contaminated by slurry leakage or pesticides. You will have an immense amount of extra work if water is not laid on to the fields, as you will have to cart water to the trough daily. However, most fields these days do have water laid on and

proper water troughs. Do not use an old bath as a trough as the sharp edges can cause injury. Fences must be well maintained and gates kept in good condition, well-hinged to solid gate posts, and kept latched and padlocked. Stabling is essential. If you do not have a stable but you do have a barn, perhaps you can construct a loose box in this. Purpose-built loose boxes can be purchased from a number of firms specialising in the supply of portable buildings. Always see the products of several firms before making a decision to buy. Sometimes it is possible to acquire a second-hand portable loose box at a fairly reasonable cost, although you will have to pay for its transport. This

New Forest Peverill Pirouette, owned by Mrs P Haycock.

must be thoroughly disinfected before it is erected. Apart from the stable you need a dry barn or shed to store feed stuffs and another for hay, straw or other bedding. You need tools for mucking out: a four-tine fork, shovel, broom and barrow.

Finally, you need a full grooming kit and tack for the pony.

Tack and shoeing

Good saddlery, or tack, is expensive. New saddles take a deal of 'breaking in' both for the pony and rider, so it is better to buy a second-hand saddle of a good British make. A reliable saddler should be willing to bring several saddles to the pony and find one that fits properly. It is essential that the saddle fits and is in good repair, as a badly-fitting saddle can gall or injure a pony's back. It is also essential that the saddle fits the rider.

When buying the pony, enquire what kind of bit it goes best in and keep to this. Bridles should be of good leather. If you buy a second-hand bridle, always unlatch all the buckles to be sure there are no worn places. It is wise to buy new, good-quality stirrup leathers and stirrups to fit your feet. Reins should be new or in good condition, and may be plain, plaited or rubber covered for a good grip. Good tack is a little more expensive but safer.

Keep your tack at home, as leaving it in a shed is an invitation to the thieves who raid stables. Do have your tack marked, so that it can be traced if it goes missing. Have your pony freeze branded for the same reason. All this must appear in your costing.

An on-going and essential expense for the pony is shoes and shoeing. Some ponies with very good feet only need trimming, but shoes are needed by those that are ridden regularly and do a certain amount of road work and/or competing.

It was well said that 'no foot, no horse', and 'for want of a nail a shoe was lost', and all the other old rhymes on the subject. Good feet and good shoeing are paramount if you want a sound, healthy pony and a safe ride. The farrier's bill is one on which you should never skimp. Shoes usually need to be renewed about every six weeks. If the pony is only in light work then for one visit it may just be 'removes'. The farrier takes the shoes off, trims the feet and puts the same set back on. This does not cost as much as a new set, but can usually be done only once with each set. Book the farrier to come regularly; do not expect to be able to ring and get him whenever you want him. A good farrier is always busy, so a regular booking will ensure that your pony's feet are kept in good order. Ask around your district and you will soon hear which farrier is the best. It will probably be the one who shoes the hunt horses, although he may be so popular that he is fully booked!

Other expenses

Having the pony on your own property and in your care entails other expenses. If you intend to compete at shows, or want to move your pony about the country to Riding Club, Pony Club and so on, you will need a trailer (and maybe a change of car to one strong enough to pull it). A trailer is best obtained from a recognised dealer that specialises in this commodity. He will have a good range of used trailers for sale, so it is not necessary to purchase a new one. Do make sure the second-hand trailer has been properly serviced. Look at the ramp both up and down, make sure the flooring is sound, try the groom's door, take a good look at tyres and hitch, and ensure everything is in good working order. If you are ignorant about these matters, ask someone knowledge-able to go with you and give advice.

However healthy and strong a pony might be, there are times when a veterinary surgeon is necessary. Again, ask among the horsey people in your neighbour-hood and the best local equine vet will soon be recommended. Keep a note of the telephone numbers of both vet and farrier near your telephone, as you never know when a crisis might occur.

Best quality hay is always the most expensive, but is by far the best buy. Cheap, poor quality hay will be unpalatable and mostly wasted, as well as having little nutritional value, and it can give the pony respiratory problems if it is dusty. Hay should be stored under cover but, if you have to stack the bales outside, put some branches down on the ground so that the lower bales can stand up out of the wet, and cover the whole with well tied-down plastic or canvas sheeting. The same goes for straw bales.

Not all stables use straw for bedding. Many use wood shavings, peat or a mixture of this and sawdust or other products. In winter always have enough of your chosen bedding in reserve in case bad weather sets in and it is in short supply or you cannot get out to collect it.

Native ponies do not need large quantities of short feed, but a certain amount is necessary, especially when the pony is in regular work. Feedstuffs should be obtained from a reliable supplier and stored in lidded, metal, rodent-proof bins. Rats and mice can be a problem so do try to protect your feedstuffs.

Bernard Tidmarsh, master farrier.

There will of course be other expenses as you go along. Your own riding apparel, bandages and boots and a summer sheet for the pony, a wool rug and an all-weather rug (called a New Zealand) and repairs to saddlery.

On the plus side, once you have a pony of your own, whatever age you are, your friends and relations will always know what to give you for Christmas, birthday or anniversary presents – something is sure to be wanted for your equine friend!

Chapter 14

Basic Management

The new pony

When your new pony is delivered to your home or the livery stables, it is wise to have it stabled for the first 24 hours so that it becomes accustomed to its new surroundings and gets to know its new keepers. When you do turn your pony out in the field, make sure that it is fitted with a comfortable and strong head collar, preferably leather. This head collar must fit properly and not be so loose that it can be pulled off or so tight that it causes sores.

At first the pony may stand away when you go to catch it as it does not know you. Do not follow it if it moves away, and never chase it if it gallops off. Take a bucket or bowl of feed with you and stay near the gate. Curiosity and greed will eventually get the better of it and it will come up. Let it get well into the feed, and rub its cheek and talk to it before taking hold of the head collar. When you have your pony safe, gently put the feed container on the ground while it is still eating and then attach the rope, which you can have tied round your waist or

Free to run, but within secure fencing.
Photograph by Tracey Elliott Reed.

over your shoulder. After a few days the pony should be quite easy to catch. It just requires patience.

Although the pony may have been wormed recently, it is advisable to do this again within the first few weeks of ownership. After this, the worming must be undertaken regularly, as otherwise the pony may get an infestation that will cause it to lose condition and can make it very ill. It is also necessary to have a worm-free pony so that the pasture where it grazes is kept clean.

Pasture

Whether you have one, two or several acres of grazing for your pony it must be properly managed. The health of the pony depends on clean grazing and an adequate water supply.

You should divide whatever pasture you own or rent into two halves so that one section can be shut up while the other is grazed; that way you will keep an even supply.

Post and rail fencing is the best and safest means of fencing for ponies, as wire can cause injury, and not all ponies will stay behind an electric fence.

Pasture must be kept clean and weed-free. Every few days, take your barrow into the field, pick up all the dung and transfer it to the muck heap. Dung left in the field can cause a build-up of worms, kills the grass, encourages rank weeds and reduces grazing.

When fields become ragged in late summer, ask a neighbouring farmer or contractor to come in and 'top' the field; this is done with a mower that takes off all the rough tufts and weeds. If your land is flinty, remove any large stones or flints each week, and especially before the mower comes in or the blades will break.

During spring and summer look out for any rank weeds. Ragwort should not be 'topped' but pulled up by hand and burned, as it is poisonous to equines. Nettles and docks should also be dug up before they spread to large areas of the field. Do not use sprays to kill the weeds.

Go round the pasture once a week to make sure there are no weak parts of the hedge or fence through which the pony can force its way out. Most hedged fields these days also have two or three strands of barbed wire against them. If this is the case in your fields, make sure there is no very low bottom strand over which the pony can catch a foot.

You should walk round the field every day, especially if it runs beside a road. Motorists do throw rubbish over hedges, broken glass has injured many a pony, and some people actually dump their grass clippings or windfall apples over the gate believing that these will prove a treat for the pony. All such items must be cleared away before the pony can eat them and make itself ill.

Any acorns should be scraped up and removed every day during the autumn. Although ponies can eat a few acorns and come to no harm, too many affect the liver and prove fatal.

After you have transferred the pony to fresh grazing, rake the grazed area with a spike harrow to let air into the earth and stimulate new growth.

You need to empty the water troughs each month and scour and rinse them well. If piped water is laid on, make sure the compartment that houses the ball-cock is well wrapped with straw and sacking in the late autumn to prevent the system freezing up in bad weather.

Stabling

Mountain and moorland ponies thrive best out of doors, but may need to be stabled at night in very severe weather. Ponies hunting regularly can be stabled, as can ponies that are competing, but they should spend as much time in their field as possible. In spring with a fast growth of grass it is often necessary to bring the pony in for some hours each day to prevent it eating too much. In summer bring ponies in out of the heat of the sun and away from the troublesome flies during the middle part of the day.

You can learn to build your own jumping course.

Loose boxes must be kept clean and fresh. Use straw, shavings or a mixture of the latter with sawdust as bedding, and there are other beddings offered for sale. Straw is the easiest to deal with as it composts well and the resulting mulch can usually be sold. Shavings and sawdust take several years to rot down and there is little call for this type of waste.

A tidy muck heap should be made away from the stable, preferably on a concrete base. Build a good wall of muck and then fill in the centre so it forms a square. Sweep up all manure and bits of hay and straw. Scrub out the water bowls or buckets daily, and give fresh water two or three times a day or whenever the receptacle is empty. A fixed water bowl is preferable, but if you have to use a bucket put it in the corner on the same side as the door and do not have the hay net hanging over it. Mangers or feed bowls must be scrubbed, as the residue of short feed left in the rim or corners ferments easily and will contaminate fresh feed.

A fixed manger is best for short feed but, if there is no manger, a metal or plastic bowl can be used. This should be removed as soon as the pony has cleaned up the feed, as the pony will only kick the bowl about and break it, and may injure a leg.

Haynets should be fixed to a ring high on the wall and tied tightly, as the pony may get a leg entangled if the net is hanging too low.

There should be a ring in the wall to which the pony can be tied and this should be near the haynet ring, so that the pony can nibble hay when standing in.

Native ponies need plenty of air, so if the pony is in at night it is better to put an extra rug or two on it in cold weather rather than shut the top door and run the risk of respiratory trouble. Only in driving snow or severe gales should the top door be shut.

Basic rules for mucking out are: flip clean straw against the wall and remove all dung and wet straw with the fork. Pile it in a barrow and take it to the muck heap. Spread the remaining clean straw in the stable. If the pony is to lie in at night make a proper bed of straw, which should be deep in the middle and piled about 45cm (18in) high round the walls.

'Skipping' can be done whenever you see dung in the box. The pile is removed with two boards used like two shovels, or by a four-tine prong (fork). The cleaner you keep the stable, the less bedding you use and the cleaner the pony stays.

Feeding and watering

Ask the pony's previous owner how it has been fed, with what proprietary brands of short feed and how much. Keep to this until you have gained enough experience to change diets.

Haynets should be tightly filled and dunked in the water butt and then shaken before being tied in the box. This removes any dust in the hay. Always water the pony before feeding.

Grooming

In winter ponies living out need to have good deep coats. Dried mud should be removed with a dandy brush when the ponies are brought in.

Deep coats always contain a great deal of dust so the body brush will only bring this to the surface. Brush legs and heads with the body brush. Brush mud from the mane and tail, and then comb them with the mane comb. Whether the pony is stabled or coming in from the field you should pick out its feet twice daily with the hoof pick.

In summer, ponies should be groomed with the body brush and finished with a silk cloth. Strapping with a hay wisp will bring up muscle tone. Do not wash wet mud off ponies' legs when they come in from exercising; let it dry and then brush it off. Ponies being hunted or exercised in very muddy conditions should have grease smeared on their legs and heels before they go out as this helps to prevent mud fever or cracked heels.

Although you may see other ponies clipped out in winter, it is not necessary or, indeed, wise to clip your native pony unless it is to be fully stabled. Native ponies are best out in the field and need their winter coats. Should you be riding regularly or hunting during the cold weather, a 'gullet', or 'trace' clip can be done. The former is just a strip clipped on the underside of the neck to the breast-bone, the latter comes half way up the pony's body leaving the belly clear of hair.

Ideally native ponies should carry their full coat, which will moult out in spring, leaving a shining jacket. The summer coat can be groomed with a body brush.

Do not attempt to remove a shoe if it works loose or the clenches (nails) rise, but ask the farrier to call. In an emergency your farrier will nearly always be able to stop off on his way to another client.

Poisonous weeds and trees

Trees: yew, laburnum, box, laurel, rhododendron.
Plants: ragwort, foxglove, deadly nightshade, aconite, lupin, delphinium, meadow saffron, white and green hellebore, monkshood, henbane, spotted hemlock, thorn apple.

Garden clippings should not be fed to ponies. If a few windfall apples are mixed with the feed, they should be cut in slices.

Problems and ailments

Should the pony show any signs of distress, such as stamping, kicking or biting at the belly, rolling the eyes or sweating, send at once for the veterinary surgeon, as this sort of behaviour suggests that the pony is suffering either from colic or from poison. Whilst waiting for the vet, keep the pony walking outside – do not allow it to lie down. If it is raining throw a rug over its back.

Sometimes a pony gets 'cast' in its box. It lies down in a poor position, usually with its legs too close to the wall, and then cannot get up. The pony thrashes around

ponies. No lame pony should be ridden. Ponies can contract ringworm, usually from fences that infected cattle have rubbed against. It shows itself in round, bare patches on the skin and needs to be treated immediately.

Ponies can contract lice, usually in their manes. Use a louse wash to remove the pests as they can debilitate the pony.

Owning a pony can be a family affair. Welsh Section B Breccles Yellow and family.

and may panic. Two or more adults can usually pull the pony round and steady it until it can get to its feet. If it is very agitated and sweating, walk it about for a while until it settles and then offer a drink of warmed water.

Ponies may get lame for a variety of reasons: a pinching shoe, a stone in the foot, tendon trouble, a knock, a bad splint and so on. New owners are advised always to seek veterinary advice for lame

Keep a check on the pony's teeth; they may get sharp edges, and older ponies often get ragged teeth. The veterinary surgeon should examine the teeth at regular intervals and file them when necessary.

As a pony owner you need to use your eyes and ears to ensure that your equine companion remains healthy and sound, so that it can give you years of work and pleasure.

Chapter 15

Shows and Showing

If you intend to show a mountain and moorland pony, it is essential to ensure that your animal is registered with its breed society. You will be given the pony's registration papers by its previous owner, and you must then transfer the pony to your name, using the form issued by the appropriate society. Once the pony has been transferred to your name, you can enter it in classes for the breed. It is important to give the pony's registered name and its registration number when filling in entry forms.

Entry into the show world, for the newcomer at least, is best made at small local events. These are held up and down the country from March to October, and are aimed at local riders of all ages. Newer adult riders will find a class to suit them and their mounts, and the experience gained at these enjoyable, low profile events provides valuable knowledge for larger shows later on.

Young people who join the Pony Club will find that their branch runs at least one

Welsh Cob Section C Synod Roy Rogers with owner/breeder Mr Cerdin Jones. No matter how good the pony's conformation, a smart turn-out of both horse and handler is essential.

show, and they will also get experience at rallies and the annual camp.

In most areas, gymkhanas are held all through the summer months, and fun rides all year.

For adult riders, joining a Riding Club can provide a fund of experience. Most clubs hold at least one show during the season.

The next level is the local horse and pony show or small agricultural show, where there is a broader classification. There may be an affiliation to one or both of the main pony societies, the National Pony Society and the Ponies Association UK (formerly Ponies of Britain), where qualifying competitions for the annual championships are held.

Then there are the shows held by the breed societies, where entry is restricted to that particular breed. Always well classified and well organised, they are a 'must' for the new owners in a breed for it is here, among the experienced pony people and the top class stock on parade, that you will gain knowledge. Whether you go just to look or take the plunge and enter a class or two, these events are not to be missed. Most breed societies now have enthusiasts' clubs, and these also run shows, fun rides and seminars which are popular and well-supported and which provide both education and entertainment.

Larger shows confined solely to mountain and moorland breeds, such as the East Anglian Native Pony Show, put on classes for all native breeds and classes to suit all ages and stages of experience.

The county shows, such as Newark and Notts, Three Counties, Cheshire County, Shropshire & West Midlands and so on, all schedule some of the native breeds, while such events as the Royal Show, Royal Windsor, Royal Lancs, Bath and West, Great Yorkshire, East of England and the Royal Highland bring competition of the highest level.

For all competitive native pony owners, the climax of the season comes in August with the National Pony Society's two-day summer show held on the show ground at Malvern in Worcestershire, and the four-day summer show held on the East of England show ground at Peterborough by the Ponies Association UK. Both shows attract entries from all over the United Kingdom.

The year draws to an exciting climax with the final of the Mountain and Moorland ridden championships held at the Christmas show at Olympia.

It is important that newer riders do not over-reach themselves by entering classes at large shows for which neither they nor their pony are ready and for which they have no notion of what is required for the turn-out of pony or rider. This can only lead to embarrassment and disillusionment as well as disappointment.

For small local events, study your local paper, where most are advertised, and also watch for fly posters in the area.

Established shows, breed shows and large, local shows are advertised in the special show editions of *Horse and Hound* published on the first three weekends in March.

For newcomers to the native pony scene, it is valuable to attend some large shows and observe the type of winning pony, how it is produced and ridden, and the turn-out of both the pony and rider. Watch how the judge deals with the entry, what the ponies are expected to do and how the riders respond to the judge's instructions. Watch the in-hand classes because, by observing the ponies carefully, you will learn more about the make, shape, movement and characteristics of your particular breed.

Showing can involve the whole family and is a very enjoyable day out for all.

Showing for the younger child

The youngest riders compete in the leading rein classes which are tremendously popular and always well filled. These are for ponies of four years and over; the age of the rider varies with the different societies, but rarely exceeds nine years and is usually eight years, and many riders start very young indeed. The mountain and moorland leading rein is open to the small breeds. Ponies in this must not exceed 12.0 hh so Welsh Sections A and B, the smallest of the New Forest ponies, Dartmoor and Shetland are the usual entrants. Exmoor ponies, because of their build, are not suitable for very tiny riders. The ponies have to be led by a dismounted attendant and all are asked to walk together in a wide circle round the ring. The class is halted and each rider trots the pony across the judge's field of vision. When this is completed the ponies circle again, then the judge pulls in the ponies in order of preference and asks each to give a short show at walk and trot.

At the big shows the judge may ask for the little riders to dismount and the ponies to be 'stripped', that is, have their saddles removed, and be run out in-hand by the leader.

Never be dismayed or stop trying if you and your young charge are pulled in down the line. If you give a very good individual show and the judge likes the pony better on closer examination, you may come further up in the placings.

At most shows a rosette is given to every participant as an encouragement. It avoids disappointment and makes the tiny rider eager to try again.

When the child has learned to ride off the lead rein, the next class is First Ridden. The rider must be 12 years or under and again the pony must be one of the small breeds. Ponies walk and trot as a class, but are required to canter in the individual show.

Once the child is riding well and has learned to jump small obstacles safely, the little courses of natural jumps put up for the Nursery Stakes and Cradle Stakes prove very exciting and enjoyable.

Young children love the Fancy Dress classes held at small country shows, and often there are gymkhana classes on the lead rein. However, always take care that your enthusiasm as a leader anxious for your charge to win a rosette does not make the small rider frightened or even fall off.

Mountain and moorland breed classes

At large shows the mountain and moorland breeds have their own section with both in-hand and riding classes. The in-hand section has classes for yearlings, two- and three-year olds, and four years and over. Sometimes the stallions have a class to themselves, and mares and geldings are usually classified together. The ridden classes are for stallions, mares and geldings.

There are usually classes for any breed of registered native pony, and these are divided into sections for small and large breeds. Again, ridden classes for mixed native breeds are for stallions, mares and geldings.

In these mixed breed classes there will be two, three or even four sections, depending on the size of the show and which society's rules the show is held under. Such divisions may be:

A: Small breeds
Dartmoor, Exmoor, Shetland, Welsh Sections A and B

B: Large breeds
Dales, Fell, Connemara, New Forest, Highland

C: Large breeds
Welsh Sections C and D

Sometimes the Connemara and New Forest have a separate section, and often the Welsh Cobs are classified with other large breeds. The Welsh B may have a separate class or A and B are put together. When entering any of these classes check your schedule carefully to see that you are in the right section. Mixed in-hand classes are classified in the same way. The class walks, trots and canters together on both reins, which means that when the paces have been seen in one direction, the ponies are pulled back to a walk, then cross the ring at a trot and lead off in a circle in the opposite direction. The judge pulls in the ponies in order, and then each rider and pony must give an individual show, usually at the direction of the judge. The rider is expected to gallop the pony in this part of the class.

Often, ponies have to be stripped and run out in hand before they are re-mounted, and are then walked in a circle for the judge to select the final line up.

There are popular mountain and moorland Working Hunter classes which are divided into breeds as with the ridden classes. These are judged in two sections.

The jumping comes first, and any pony with a clear round or one with a few

Menai Furious, ridden by Kath Girdler, displays typical balance and action.

faults comes back for the judging of conformation. Marking is on style of riding, control of pony, breed type and conformation, with up to 50 points for the jumping section. The pony with the highest number of points is the winner. Riders of any age can take part in any novice or open class for natives under saddle, unless there is a stipulation in the schedule.

Other classes

Breeds such as the Welsh Sections A and B, New Forest and Connemara can find success in the Show Hunter Pony classes, which are ridden on the flat but are scheduled for ponies that have more bone than the average show pony. All breeds can go in show jumping classes confined to ponies, but be sure to check the height allowed in each class before entering.

There are many other scheduled classes that can be entered by owners of native ponies, such as Working or Handy Pony, Family Pony, Best Turned Out, Equitation, and so on.

Working or Handy Pony classes contain a number of obstacles that pony and rider have to negotiate, and the hazards may include jumping in and out of a jumping lane with a bend in it, leading over a 'bridge', dismounting and taking a pole down before re-mounting, jumping the rest of the obstacle and dis-mounting to replace the pole, and opening and shutting a gate while mounted.

In Handy Pony the mounted rider is often asked to collect an item from one side of the ring and take it to the other side. This can be a bucket, a filled hay net, a coat or a horse rug. Some of these classes end with the rider having to dismount and lead the pony through a front and rear loading trailer.

Family Pony Classes are for really reliable ponies that any member of the family can sit on safely, and some classes call for two riders of different ages from the same family to take part. The pony must be rock steady and willing, may have to jump a small obstacle and have riders mounting and dismounting from both sides. Classes for Best Rider scheduled as Equitation classes, are divided according to the age of the rider.

Apart from spring and summer shows the autumn heralds the Hunter Trials. These are held in most country districts, some run by breed societies, others by hunts or show societies. They are held over a natural course of jumps across fields and are great fun for both pony and rider. There are usually classes for those under and over a certain age limit (16 or sometimes 18), and a novice class with smaller fences over a shorter course.

Langfield Canth, an example of a top-class Dartmoor pony.

Correct clothing

Although you may hack out in jeans and an anorak it is necessary to be properly clothed when competing. It is not essential to have a navy or black jacket although many riders do wear them. A well-cut hacking jacket of a quiet pattern of tweed is very smart and looks right on a native breed. A hard hat is essential, and must match the standard required by the regulations. Children must wear hats with chin straps attached and correctly adjusted. A shirt and tie, jodhpurs and jodhpur boots complete the outfit. Some adults prefer breeches and boots but these can look rather overdone on a native pony. Avoid a plastic buttonhole – a small real cornflower or rosebud looks better if you must wear one.

Do not wear a stock or cravat as these are too fussy for such classes. A collar and tie is quite appropriate. The tie's colour should match the jacket. Women and girls should always wear a hairnet. Gloves, either leather or string-backed, complete a neat ensemble. No spurs are allowed in native ridden classes, and only a show cane should be carried.

In leading rein classes, the leader should be smart but not fussy and both sexes should wear a hat. Men can wear a bowler, trilby or cap. Women should wear a well-fitting hat that will not blow off, such as a neat velvet beret or a pull-on felt. Either sex can wear a panama in the summer months.

Gentlemen can wear a suit, usually grey or navy striped, or cavalry twill or cord trousers with a hacking jacket. Ladies should wear sensible footwear, as so many showgrounds are muddy or soft and high heels soon sink in. Avoid fussy skirts with swirling loose panels, elbow length gloves or hats piled with flowers.

Many mothers like to colour co-ordinate their outfit with the pony and rider and this can be very effective. Professional lady handlers usually wear riding clothes but with a pull-on felt hat instead of their hard hat.

Go prepared for rain; there is a wide range of smart short or long waterproof and waxed coats, some with matching hats.

Small girl riders should have their hair tied back neatly with hair ribbons. Large bunches of gaudy ribbons floating in the breeze give an untidy appearance. Most

Shetland Bincombe Volunteer shows off his rosettes.

ponies wear plaited velvet brow bands in two colours, one of which should match the hair ribbons and perhaps the trim on the mother's clothes and hat. It is necessary to give a harmonious whole to the picture of handler, rider and pony – one should not overshadow the other.

Small boys often like to wear a bowler hat, but this too must be secured with a chin strap. Both the leaders and the small riders should wear gloves.

Leading rein riders should not carry whips. The class for Best Turned Out means that pony, tack and rider all must be clean and neat. Little touches, such as the wearing of an invisible hair net by the females, the polishing of the instep of the

Ceulan Cariad, owned by Dr Wynne Davies, displays spectacular movement.

boots and the type of gloves worn, can mean the difference between a place and relegation. The standard in such classes can be very high but do not think that you need to have all new tack and clothes to go top of the line. Good quality leather that has been well kept and is soft and supple, and a clean, neat rider together with a well-groomed pony are more likely to catch the eye of the discerning judge.

The pony's turn-out

Mountain and moorland ponies must not have their manes or tails plaited for their breed classes, but must be shown with both well brushed. It is permitted for New Forest, Connemara, Dartmoor and Welsh Section B to have their manes pulled to a moderate length, so that these can be plaited when competing in classes other than those for native breeds. Ponies must not enter the ring in bandages or boots. The only decorations allowed are for the Welsh breeds, which can be shown with a small plait made from the first hairs in the mane behind the ear, and the Dales, which are allowed to have a bunch of ribbons plaited into the top of their tails.

Tack

Always ride your pony in the bit it is used to wearing. Some riders have been known to put the pony in a double bridle for the class when it has never worn one before, and then wonder why they cannot get a performance out of it. If you decide your pony is ready for a double and you are capable of using one correctly, then make sure the pony is thoroughly used to the new bridle by the time it goes in the ring.

In ridden classes martingales are rather out of place. A running martingale is acceptable but a standing martingale is not. In show classes the pony should wear an ordinary nose band, not a drop noseband or one with a sheepskin covering. If you use a girth of nylon or similar material, avoid bright colours, and do not have glaring saddle cloths embroidered with your initials.

The saddle should have been chosen to fit both the pony and yourself, but if a numnah is needed, choose one that fits neatly and does not stand out and spoil the line. Tiny children may feel safer if the pony is fitted with a neck strap which they can hold when they have to trot. Do not go in for gimmicks or try to emulate the riders seen on television; they are all very experienced and if they use a new gadget it is because they have proved it will suit their animal and make it perform better. A pony can easily be ruined by being forced to wear a bit that does not suit it, or being roped in by a new type of rein or given a different nose band. Make sure that the bit fits the pony's mouth, that it is not too tight and pinching the corners, or too large and hanging loosely. Make sure the bridle is the right size and correctly adjusted. When you first start going to shows you will find other competitors very helpful if you ask for advice on these matters.

Pegasus! Your mountain and moorland pony will be ready for any fancy dress fun!

Preparing for the show

If you get the showing 'bug', it helps to have a box or case for each rider kept ready for the show to avoid anything being left behind. A label stuck on the lid can give a list of contents: hat, gloves, tie, hair nets, ribbons, cane, spare socks/tights, safety pins, cottons and needles, and so on. Everyone attending a show should have a small first-aid box, although the St John's Ambulance or a similar organisation is present at all reputable shows.

You should assemble a tack box for the pony, so that you can safely pack all the things you may need at a show the night before. Hoof pick, mane comb, brushes, hoof oil and brush, vaseline, bandages, spare girth, scissors, plaiting thread and needles if you intend to go in open classes, are just some of the items you will need. Overhaul and clean the tack the day before the show, making sure that reins, leathers and girths are secure and not worn or frayed. Make a cover for your saddle so that it does not get scratched in transit and wrap bridles in a towel.

It is essential to adopt a philosophical attitude to showing. You will not always be in the ribbons and it is best to accept this fact from the start of your career. Go intending to enjoy yourself and to learn something from each event. That way you will truly come to love your showing days.

For information on the Two Day Summer show, apply to the Secretary of the National Pony Society. For information on the shows organised by Ponies Association UK, including its four-day summer show, again apply to the Secretary. You can find both organisations listed in **Useful Addresses**.

The flag bearers. Welsh Cobs Section D and their riders set the standard. Photograph by Pleasure Prints

Useful Addresses

In each instance, please address your enquiry to the Society's Secretary.

Dales Pony Society
Greystones
Gleve Avenue
Great Longstone
Bakewell
Derbyshire DE45 1TY

The Dartmoor Pony Society
Pizewell Farm
Yelverton
Devon PL20 6TN

English Connemara Pony Society
Woodlands
St Mary's Cottage
Woodlands St Mary
Lambourn
Oxon

The Exmoor Pony Society
Glen Fern
Widdicombe
Dulverton
Somerset TA22 2RY

Fell Pony Society
Riccarton Mill
Newcastleton
Roxburghshire TD9 0SN

Highland Pony Society
Beechwood
Elie
Fife KY9 1DH
Scotland

The National Pony Society
Willingdon House
102 High Street
Alton
Hampshire GU34 1EN
Tel: 01420 88333

New Forest Pony and Cattle Breeding Society
Beacon Cottage
Burley
Ringwood
Hampshire BH24 4EW

Ponies Association UK
Chesham House
56 Green End Road
Sawtry
Huntingdon
Cambs PE17 5UY
Tel: 01487 830278

Shetland Pony Stud Book Society
Pedigree House
6 King's Place
Perth PH2 8AD
Scotland

Welsh Pony and Cob Society
6 Chalybeate Street
Aberystwyth
Dyfed SY23 1HS
Wales

Suggested Reading

Cox, Maurice, *The Shetland Pony*, published by A C Black & Co. Last edition 1976, now out of print but can occasionally be obtained from bookshops such as The Landsman's Library, which specialises in country publications

Davies, Wynne, *Welsh Ponies and Cobs*, J A Allen

Davies, Wynne, *The Welsh Mountain Pony*, J A Allen

English Connemara Pony Society, *The Connemara Chronicle*

Hulme, Susan, *Native Ponies of the British Isles*

Lyne, Pat, *Shrouded in Mist* and *Out of the Mist*, published by Miss Lyne, the breed historian of the Connemara pony

Palmer, Joseph, *The Dartmoor Pony: A History of the Breed*, Devon Books

Polling, Elizabeth, *The Exmoor Pony*, the official handbook of the Society

Richardson, Clive, *The Fell Pony*, J A Allen

Russell, Valerie, *The New Forest Pony*

Speed, J G and Speed, M G, *The Exmoor Pony: its origins and characteristics*

Summerhayes Encyclopaedia for Horsemen

For the Highland pony, there is a northern breed publication, *The Highland Gazette*, obtainable through the Society, while the Enthusiasts' Club produces a quarterly booklet called *Highland Times*. Both are full of information about the breed and also publish a sales list.

Glossary
of Everyday Terms

Action
Movement of the pony.

Aged
Ponies over seven years of age.

Agisters
Those employed by the Verderers in the New Forest to look after the care and welfare of animals grazing on the Forest and to collect annual payments for such rights.

Aids
The signals by which the rider communicates with the pony.

Backing
A stage in the training of the pony when the trainer first gets on its back.

Balance
The pony carries its own weight and that of the rider in such a way that it can go easily and comfortably at all paces.

Bandages
There are a number of different types of bandage. Most used are the tail bandage that keeps the hair on the pony's tail smooth, and travelling bandages for all

New Forest ponies are rounded up before being sent to the Beaulieu Road Sales.

four legs when the animal is in transit. There are also exercise bandages, stable bandages and bandages used for various leg troubles.

Bars (of the mouth)
The spaces either side of a pony's mouth between the tushes and the molar teeth, on which the bit lies.

Beaulieu Road Sales
Where New Forest ponies are sold at auction. They are held several times a year under the auspices of the New Forest Pony and Cattle Breeding Society.

Bedded down
The pony's bed is set and made comfortable for the night.

Bedding
There are various products sold on which ponies may be bedded down in stable, including straw, shavings, sawdust, moss peat and dried bracken.

Behind the bit
This term refers to when the pony shakes its head, appears to be frightened of the bit and does not want to take pressure on the bars. There are several reasons for this: wrong bitting, a sore mouth or tooth trouble are just three. Expert advice should be sought.

Bit
The metal piece that goes in the pony's mouth and is held in place by the straps of the bridle. There are many kinds of bit, but the most useful and usual for ponies are the *snaffle*, which comes in several types, or one of the *pelhams*. Bits should be removed after use and well washed and dried.

Bit shields
Circular pieces of leather placed at either end of the bit to prevent galling of the lips.

Bolting
This is when a pony gallops out of control. Habitual bolters are dangerous.

Bone
The measurement of the bone of a pony is taken below the knee and the hock.

Branding
Marking a pony with a hot branding iron. New Forest and Exmoor are two of the breeds branded. New Forest ponies carry their owner's brand; Exmoors are branded with the herd and herd number.

Cast
A pony is said to be cast if it gets down too near the sides of a loose box and cannot scramble up. It needs help to get to its feet as quickly as possible.

Casting coat
A pony will cast its coat in autumn and spring.

Cavaletti
Low movable wooden jumps over which ponies can be schooled. They are loose poles 2.7m (9ft) long placed on Xs at either end. The poles can also be placed on the ground for use as trotting poles. Work over these helps to balance both pony and rider.

Chin groove
The small depression found under the lower lip in which the curb chain lies.

Clipping
The removal by electric clippers of

unwanted coat. To be true to their breed, native ponies should not be clipped but some, such as Welsh Section B, Connemara and New Forest that take part in open competition, are clipped for shows in the early spring. Ponies that hunt usually have a trace clip, that is, the belly is clipped as high as the elbow, so that they do not get overheated.

Clothing

All items such as rugs used for ponies are referred to as 'horse clothing'.

Cold back

This term refers to a pony that objects to the pressure of the saddle when it is first put on. It can help if you warm its back by placing a rug over it for half an hour before saddling, or even by warming the saddle. Ponies with cold back should be saddled and lightly girthed, and left in the stable until they are relaxed before being mounted, otherwise they may buck.

Colours

Colours found in ponies are as follows: bay; brown; black; chestnut; liver chestnut; grey; dun; blue roan; strawberry roan; piebald (black and white); skewbald (brown and white); palomino; cream. Shetland ponies are the only native breed where piebald and skewbald are allowed, and blue-eyed creams are not allowed in the New Forest pony.

Colt

A male horse or pony up to the age of four years.

Corns

Corns can make the pony lame. Usually they are caused by bad shoeing or shoes that have been left on too long.

Covered school

A large building in which riding lessons are given and ponies schooled.

Dock

That part of the tail on which the hair grows as well as the bare underside.

Donkey foot

An upright narrow foot with a pinched-in heel and contracted frog. Also referred to as a 'boxy' foot. This type of foot is not to be encouraged.

Dorsal stripe or Eel stripe

A continuous black, brown or dun stripe down the pony's back from the base of the mane to the tail. Typical of the Highland ponies.

Farrier

The farrier shoes horses and ponies.

Fat

No pony should be allowed to get too fat. Over-fat ponies tend to have all manner of ills and trouble with wind and/or heart, but mostly suffer from laminitis (fever in the feet).

Favouring a leg

When the pony fails to place the weight on all four limbs equally but appears to be favouring one. This means it is lame. It is also referred to as 'going short'.

Feet

These are the most important part of the pony and should always have the greatest attention paid to them. Regular shoeing is essential. The pony's best friend is a competent farrier. There is an old saying, 'no foot, no horse' – it is very true. Check your pony's feet regularly.

Filly
A female pony under the age of four years.

Fly caps
Made of netting, they can be worn over the pony's ears as a protection against flies. They should not be worn in the ring.

Fodder or forage
Refers to any feeding stuffs fed to ponies. Short feed refers to pony nuts, chaff, oats and so on.

Frog
The V-shaped formation in the sole of the foot which carries the weight of the horse. It is elastic and expands laterally.

Frost nails
These can be fixed to the shoes by the farrier to prevent the pony slipping in frosty weather.

Girth
The girth can be made of leather, nylon or webbing. It goes under the pony's belly and keeps the saddle firmly in place.

Girth galls
Sores under the girth. Caused by ill-fitting or wrongly adjusted girths.

Grass
Nature's balanced ration for the pony. Grassland should be kept in clean condition and not overgrazed. Native ponies should not have access to too much good grazing for too long at a time. Other feeds must supplement the grass ration when the pony is in regular work.

Grooming
Regular grooming keeps the coat and skin in good order. The basic grooming kit comprises body brush, curry comb, dandy brush, mane comb, hoof pick, sponges, hoof oil and brush and stable rubber. Other items may be added as the need arises.

Hand
Ponies and horses are measured by 'hands'. Each 'hand' measures 10cm (4in). The EEC now requires equines to be measured in centimetres.

Hay net
A net made of cord which, when filled, is tied up in the box so that the pony can help itself.

Head collar
Sometimes referred to as a head stall, it is made of leather, webbing or several other new materials in bright colours. The best are made of good leather with brass fittings.

Head collar rope
A stout rope with a strong metal clip affixed to one end. The clip is fastened to the head collar. Used for leading or for tying the pony securely when it is in its horse box or stable.

In front of the bit
Said of a horse that hangs on the hand and pulls.

In-hand
Classes in the show ring for led ponies, either wearing bridle or head collar. The in-hand classes are divided into young stock and senior stock classes.

Iron
The stirrup iron.

Jibbing
A bad and rather dangerous habit when a pony refuses to go forward and in some cases runs backward.

Keepers
Leather loops to retain the straps on a bridle.

Knee caps
Made of leather stitched to felt and worn by ponies in transit to prevent injury. The top strap is fastened tighter than the lower one.

Lameness
Can be caused by any one of a number of things. Seek veterinary advice.

Leading rein
The leading rein can be of narrow leather or webbing. It has a buckle at one end that fastens to the pony's bridle; the other end is held by the person who is to lead a pony being ridden by a small child either during early lessons or in classes for leading rein ponies at shows.

Leathers
The stirrup leathers.

Livery stable
A professionally-run establishment which specialises in taking and looking after other people's horses and ponies.

Loose box
The average size is about 3 x 3m (10 x 10ft) for a pony but may be larger by 60cm (2ft). The pony can be left loose or be tied up as desired.

Measuring stick
A device for measuring horses and ponies. It is marked in 'hands'.

Mucking out
General term for cleaning out stables.

Nappy
A stubborn or bad tempered pony is referred to as nappy if it refuses the aids, or if it will not leave the stable or the company of the other ponies with whom it lives or is alongside in a show ring.

Near side
The left side of the pony when viewed from the rear. Mounting is usually accomplished from the near side, but it is useful to accustom the pony to be mounted from either side.

Neck strap
A strap fastened around the pony's neck, useful for very young or novice riders, who can hold on to it and thus avoid hurting the pony's mouth by clutching at the reins suddenly for support.

Off side
The right hand side of the pony when viewed from the rear.

On the bit
When a pony takes a light but definite feel of the bit.

One day event
Consisting of dressage, cross country and show jumping. Many are held during the year. The Pony Club has a very successful ODE competition.

Over-bent
Exaggerated head carriage when the chin is tucked into the chest.

Over-reaching
The inner rim of the toe of the hind shoe strikes the heel of the front foot.

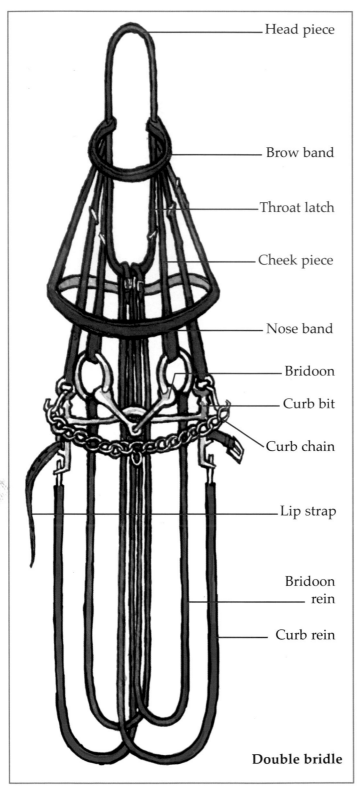

— Head piece

— Brow band

— Throat latch

— Cheek piece

— Nose band

— Bridoon

— Curb bit

— Curb chain

— Lip strap

Bridoon
— rein

— Curb rein

Double bridle

Head collar

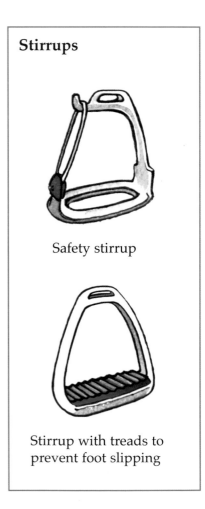

Stirrups

Safety stirrup

Stirrup with treads to
prevent foot slipping

Right: Snaffle bridle
Suitable for well-schooled ponies and riders of all ages, particularly novice and small riders.

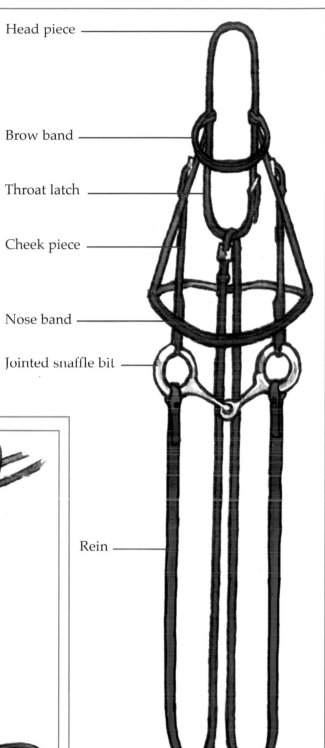

Head piece

Brow band

Throat latch

Cheek piece

Nose band

Jointed snaffle bit

Rein

Running martingale gives moderate control

Over-reach boot
Made of rubber or plastic, sometimes laced, to be worn on the front feet to prevent injury from over-reaching.

Over-ride
Term used in the show ring when one rider deliberately passes another on the inside nearest the judge.

Paddock
A small field of sweet herbage with a good, clean water supply and safe fencing.

Parrot mouth
This is when the top jaw protrudes over the lower and is often referred to as 'overshot'. It prevents the pony from grazing properly and the inability to eat properly can lead to digestive troubles.

Pin toes
When the pony stands with its feet pointing towards each other.

Plaits
Sometimes referred to as braids. A native pony may not be plaited for the show ring but must be shown with free mane and tail. The Welsh breeds may have one small plait made from the first hairs of the mane behind the ear.

Pricked foot
If a nail has been driven into the sensitive area of the foot and the pony has gone lame, it is said to have been 'pricked'.

Pulled tail and mane
The loose, straggly hairs at the top of a tail are pulled to give a clean, smooth effect. Rough and raggy manes can be pulled in Welsh Section B, Connemara and the New Forest, as these breeds are often shown in open classes where they may need to be

plaited. Novices should not try to pull manes and tails until they have been properly instructed in the art.

Quarter marks
Fancy patterns made with brush and comb on the rumps of ponies going in the show ring.

Rasp
A long-handled metal file used for rasping teeth. It is advised to engage a veterinary surgeon to undertake this important task.

Red ribbon
If a pony is known to kick, a small red ribbon should be plaited into the top of the tail as a warning to others not to get too close. This is especially important in the hunting field.

Ribbons
A popular term for the rosettes won at shows. 'In the ribbons' is the term used about successful horses and riders.

Rig
A male who has a retained testicle or who has been improperly gelded. A rig can be dangerous.

Risen clench
When a clench (nail) rises on the pony's hoof due to wear. This should be attended to by the farrier as soon as possible.

Roller
A form of girth made of leather, hemp and webbing used to keep a day or night rug in place.

Round-up
This takes place on moor and mountain at certain times of the year, when the ponies ranging free can be brought in for the

owners to sort out, and also for branding, worming, and so on.

Rug
There are many different kinds of rug. Day rugs and night rugs, paddock sheets, quilted rugs, sweat sheets, and so on. New Zealand rugs are made of waterproof materials to enable ponies to stay dry and warm when grazing out in bad weather.

Rugged up
A term applied to a pony wearing a day or night rug. It is important that rugs fit correctly and are not girthed too tightly.

Run-up
A pony is said to be run-up when it is tucked up and hollow in the loin and the ribs are showing. This condition denotes either insufficient food or ill health. Sometimes an excessive worm infestation can cause a pony to be run up. Over work, insufficient rest, inadequate time for watering and feeding can also cause a pony to run up. The condition should be dealt with speedily.

Saddle bracket
A bracket on which the saddle rests. The bracket can be fixed to a wall.

Saddlery
A term for saddles and bridles.

Safety stirrups
These have a quick release so that the foot can be freed in an emergency. Very useful for use with small children.

Salt lick
A salt block fixed in a metal holder so that the pony can lick the salt when it feels the need. Ponies need to have access to this or a lump of rock salt for their well-being.

Shelter
An open-sided shelter should be provided in the field so that ponies can get away from the sun and flies. They will rarely go in out of the rain, but may use the shelter in winter if a gale blows.

Shying
A dangerous vice, especially on our busy roads. A pony may jump back from something in the hedge, moving animals or an unfamiliar object. Sometimes caused by defective hearing or sight, usually it is the result of nervousness.

Skip
A container to hold the dung. Dung should be removed from a loose box as soon as it is deposited. The action of removing dung during the day is referred to as 'skipping', not to be confused with 'mucking out'.

Silage
Very good silage is now made for the equine market. It has good nutritional value.

Sock
A white marking extending from the coronet as far as the fetlock joint.

Spurs
No spurs are allowed to be worn by riders in mountain and moorland competitions.

Stale
The act of equine urination.

Stallion
A pony over four years of age that has not been gelded; an entire horse or pony.

Star
Any white mark on the forehead.

Star gazer
A pony which holds its head too high and is liable to jump blindly. Can be dangerous.

Staring coat
The coat stands away from the body if the pony is unwell.

Stirrup iron
The metal fitting on the stirrup leather into which the rider's foot is placed.

Stocking
White markings on a pony's leg from the coronet to the knee.

Strapping
Grooming the pony.

Stripe
A narrow white marking down the pony's face.

Tack
General name for saddles and bridles.

Tail guard
This is a cover that can be affixed to the pony's dock to prevent the tail being knocked and damaged during transit. Usually it is made of leather, but other materials can be used.

Teeth
In each jaw there are six biting teeth, called incisors, and 12 grinding teeth, called molars. Between these in both jaws lie two tushes, or tusk-like teeth. These are rarely seen in mares.

Timber
Any natural fence, not coloured show-jumping fences.

Tittup
A false, fidgety, on-the-toes jiggle, not a true gait.

Toad eye
Characteristic of the Exmoor pony. See breed chapter.

Undershot
A deformity of the jaw where the bottom jaw protrudes below the upper. The pony would find difficulty in grazing.

Verderers
Persons appointed to protect the rights and privileges of Commoners (those with grazing rights) as in the New Forest. The Court of Verderers that meets in Lyndhurst is of very ancient origin.

Veterinary surgeon
All pony owners should make sure they have the services of a veterinary surgeon who understands horses and ponies. Many practices nowadays deal mainly with small animals. It is as well to enquire in your locality for the name of an equine vet.

White face
When a white marking covers the whole of the pony's forehead and down to the mouth.

Wisp
A grooming device made from hay or straw coiled in a figure-of-eight to make a pad. Used to improve the circulation.

Wither pad
Made of soft, yielding material and used under the forepart of the saddle to relieve any pressure. The need for a wither pad usually means the saddle does not fit properly.

Wolf teeth

Rudimentary teeth that sometimes occur. They erupt in front of the upper molar teeth on either side. Sometimes they can cause mouth problems.

Woolly Pony Shows

Shows held from February to April for the native breeds before they have cast their winter coats.

Worms

All ponies should be wormed at regular intervals. For novice owners, it is advisable to take the advice of the veterinary surgeon on the best method. Fields should be kept clean of dung and regularly rested and harrowed to prevent worm infestation.

Yearling

A colt or filly having attained its first but not second birthday.

Yeld mare

A Scottish term meaning a mare not in foal. At some native shows there are classes for yeld mares.

Zebra marks

Stripes seen on the limbs of some ponies, notably the Highland.

Abbreviations

Societies

NPS	National Pony Society
PAUK	Ponies Association UK
BSPS	British Show Pony Association
PC	Pony Club
BHS	British Horse Society
ABRS	Association of British Riding Schools

Shows, trials and associated activities

M & M	Mountain and Moorland
LR	Leading Rein
FR	First Ridden
SHP	Show Hunter Pony
HP	Hunter Pony
WHP	Working Hunter Pony
WP	Working Pony
FP	Family Pony
RPB	Riding Pony Breeding
HT	Hunter Trial
ODE	One Day Event

Points of the pony

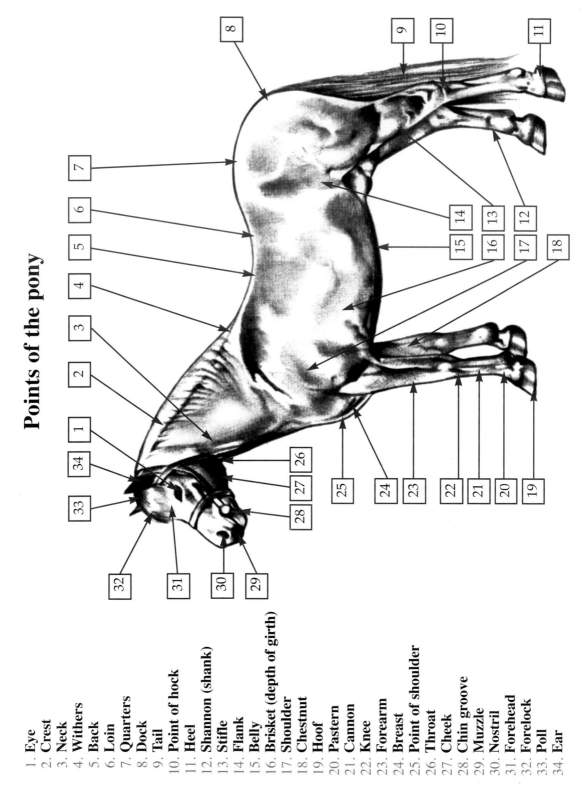

1. Eye
2. Crest
3. Neck
4. Withers
5. Back
6. Loin
7. Quarters
8. Dock
9. Tail
10. Point of hock
11. Heel
12. Shannon (shank)
13. Stifle
14. Flank
15. Belly
16. Brisket (depth of girth)
17. Shoulder
18. Chestnut
19. Hoof
20. Pastern
21. Cannon
22. Knee
23. Forearm
24. Breast
25. Point of shoulder
26. Throat
27. Cheek
28. Chin groove
29. Muzzle
30. Nostril
31. Forehead
32. Forelock
33. Poll
34. Ear